VISUAL QUICKSTART GUIDE

JAVA

FOR THE WORLD WIDE WEB

Dori Smith

Peachpit Press

Visual QuickStart Guide
Java for the World Wide Web
Dori Smith

Peachpit Press

1249 Eighth Street
Berkeley, CA 94710
(510) 524-2178
(510) 524-2221 (fax)

Find us on the World Wide Web at: http://www.peachpit.com

Peachpit Press is a division of Addison Wesley Longman

Editor: Simon Hayes
Copy Editor: Bill Cassel
Production Coordinator: Kate Reber
Compositor: Owen Wolfson
Indexer: Carol Burbo
Cover Design: The Visual Group

ISBN: 0-201-35340-7

0 9 8 7 6 5 4 3 2 1

Printed and bound in the United States of America

To Tom Negrino—not only could I not have done this book without you, but without you, I couldn't even have imagined it. Thanks for being my best friend, biggest cheerleader, and true love.

Thanks!

Thanks are especially due to my editor, Simon
Hayes, for never losing faith that a first-time
solo author really could write a readable book
about such a complex topic, and for his help
in translating Geek to English. Also, to Bill
Cassel who made sure all my i's were crossed
and my t's dotted.

To David Rogelberg and Brian Gill of Studio
B, who took one afternoon's random idea and
turned it into a book deal.

As always, to Sean Smith, World's Best Kid,™
who has patience that someday, all books will
come to an end.

Thanks to the bosses (past, present, and future)
who gave me the time and support I needed
to write this book: Doug Dawirs and Alexis
Scott of The Workbook, Steve Klinenberg and
John Lin of DigitalFacades, and Glenn Meyers
of Rare Medium. Thanks are also due to Tristan
Reid, for his help with Appendix D.

To two companies who saved me a good
deal of pain & trouble while writing this
book: Handeze, whose gloves kept this book
(unlike the last) from needing to be written
with my right arm in a cast; and Connectix,
who with Virtual PC 2 continue to prove that
one computer (with enough Mhz) is all you
need to run anything.

This book contains no coffee puns.

TABLE OF CONTENTS

TABLE OF CONTENTS

INTRODUCTION

Welcome to Java!

Java is a fairly new programming language that has achieved widespread popularity in an amazingly short amount of time. It's much simpler than many programming languages, but is extremely useful due to its cross-platform capabilities.

Most books on Java expect you to have some programming background. This book, on the other hand, doesn't make that assumption. We'll take it slow and easy, with lots of examples that build on previous examples. When you finish this book, those other books that might as well have been in Greek will now make sense.

What is Java?

Java first gained widespread notice in 1996, when it burst upon the new Internet scene with an amazing amount of hype. At the time, it wouldn't have surprised me to have seen headlines claiming that Java was the cure for cancer, or would solve world hunger.

As of this writing, the hype has died down and given rise to the perception that Java has been a flop. This couldn't be further from the truth. Java didn't fulfill all its expectations simply because nothing could have.

Java is just a programming language and, in fact, always was. What's different about Java is that it's a great programming language: very small, useful, and cross-platform. And it's not just for the Web.

Who this book is for

This book is primarily aimed at two groups of people: Web programming students and Web designers. Don't worry, though; if you're not in one of the two groups, the nice people at the bookstore won't refuse to sell it to you, and you'll probably still find it useful. However, if you are in one of these groups, you should find it right up your alley.

In any case, I've made the assumption that you already know something about the Web and HTML. For example, I'm expecting that you at least understand HTML tags well enough to be able to understand the code in your pages.

Web programming students

Thanks to the format of the Visual QuickStart Guides, many teachers have found that they make good textbooks, and the students like the price and weight.

Web designers

You learned HTML and it wasn't too hard. Then, you surprised yourself when JavaScript wasn't anywhere near as hard as you thought it would be. Now, you're wondering if maybe you should try something a little harder and check out Java. Welcome! This book will do three things for you:

◆ It will help you through learning the basics of Java, so you can see if you want to take on writing Java yourself.

◆ It will teach you the best ways to use Java programs that other people have written.

◆ It will help you talk to Java programmers in their own language. Yep, you'll learn how to speak geek with the best of 'em. I've found that people who've decided that they want to outsource their Java work are much happier with the end result when they're able to communicate with their programmers.

A note to teachers:

I'd like to collect assignments and lesson plans you've created based on this book and make them available on the Web to other teachers. Send them to me, and I'll be happy to give you credit. E-mail about the book can be sent to me at java-vqs@chalcedony.com.

A note to students:

This isn't the first book I've written that's been used as a textbook. You're not the first person to try to disguise your homework assignment as a simple question about the book. So, stop asking me, already.

About this book

This book uses some formatting tricks that should make it easier for you to understand what's going on.

In the step-by-step instructions that make up the bulk of the book, I've used a special type style to show when I'm talking about code, like this:

`<APPLET>`

`public class Applet1 extends Applet`

In the illustrations that accompany the text, I've highlighted the parts of the scripts that I'm discussing in red, so you can see at a glance what I'm referring to. Also, the important parts of the screenshots will be highlighted for clarity.

Because book pages are narrower than monitors, some of the lines of code are too long to fit on one line of the book. When this has happened, I've broken the line of code into segments and inserted an arrow to indicate that it's a continued line. Here's an example:

```
g.drawString("This is a very long message to
  display on the screen", 100 , 25);
```

Don't type that code!

Some books give you a long listing of code and expect you to type it all in. In this day and age, that's way too old-fashioned. It was hard enough for me to do the typing; you shouldn't have to do it also. So I've created a companion Web site for this book that contains all of the HTML and Java files used here, ready for you to either download or copy and paste into your own pages.

Of course, in the unlikely event that any mistakes happened to slip into print, those will be listed on the site also. You can find all this at http://www.chalcedony.com/java/

If you have any comments about this book, please send me e-mail at

java-vqs@chalcedony.com.

DON'T TYPE THAT CODE!

WHAT IS JAVA?

In 1995, the World Wide Web changed from something that only college students and a few geeks knew about into a massive fad that everyone who was anyone had to be a part of. And if you were on the Web, you had to put up your own home page, generally with an obnoxious background, an "Under Construction" graphic, and links to the three people you knew who also had pages on the Web.

Pretty soon, people said "there's gotta be more to building a Web page than this." Java hit the scene in 1995, and the Web hasn't been the same since.

A little history (and even less politics)

Several years ago (several decades in Web time) the Next Big Thing was going to be set-top boxes.

Sun Microsystems was working on a language for set-top boxes that it called Oak. In order for this new language to work, it had to be small (so that commands could quickly be sent from the cable company to your TV and vice versa) and portable (so that it would work with different cable companies). To fill the bill, James Gosling created Oak as a subset of C++.

Like most Next Big Things, set-top boxes went nowhere. But when the Web hit, Sun realized that, in Oak, they had a language that could work over the Web, allowing people to move away from those boring, static, flat pages. In a major marketing move, Sun renamed Oak "Java," and the hype began to fly.

One of the original selling points of Java was "Write Once, Run Anywhere," usually abbreviated as WORA. Sun is responsible for Java on Windows and UNIX, while Apple handles the Macintosh. Microsoft originally had a contract with Sun to work on Java, but that agreement headed to court in October 1997. Now, Microsoft sells J++ for Windows, a programming language extremely similar to Java, but with a few added benefits that work solely on Windows. For those who like to keep up with geek politics, you can follow the Java wars via these links:

http://java.sun.com/aboutJava/info/

http://www.microsoft.com/java/issues/

http://www.javalobby.org/

The Next Big Thing

There's always a Next Big Thing. Over the last few years, it's been set-top boxes, multimedia, and most spectacularly of all, push technology. NBTs make life easy on tech columnists (who just have to write about how things are going with the current NBT) and corporate MIS departments (who can always get more money out of management by claiming they're working on the current NBT). Here's a hint: almost all NBTs go nowhere.

Current NBTs, as of this writing, are portals and XML (eXtensible Markup Language)—you make the call!

Help Wanted—Creative Director

The Creative Director responds to design requests from merchandising and marketing staff for projects typically requiring fast turn around time. The Director needs to develop current in-house creative capabilities for quick-turn projects and will manage an outside agency when additional skills are needed or for longer term projects.

Current knowledge of web design technologies and ability to measure and improve site performance are critical elements of the job. The position involves significant interaction with the Engineering staff for site development, performance and production.

Reporting to the VP of Merchandise Management, the position has the following responsibilities:

Brand Image: Being the "keeper of the brand" from the creative services point of view. Translating corporate marketing strategy into site design principles and standards, appealing to a wide range of customer segments and integrating branding messages across all media, including web and print.

User Interface Design: Building a user interface with world-class site navigation, designing with a look and feel consistent with the brand, influencing buyer behavior, and basing design decisions on usability lab findings.

Qualifications: A successful Creative Director with more than five years of experience and a well-rounded portfolio, including management of a major web site. Required technical skills include copywriting, HTML, Java and PhotoShop. Additionally, proven talent in user interface design and brand marketing are critical.

Why learn Java?

Why should a non-programmer learn a programming language?

The sidebar shows one example of the many help wanted ads that have crossed my desk recently. When you read it, it's clear that the opening is for a design/marketing person, until you get to the last paragraph. Along with everything else this company wants, the requirements state that the candidate must know Java.

More and more, creatives are being asked to understand the technical side of Web design. It's not enough, as it was in the good/bad old days of print, to be able to design a page in QuarkXPress. Now, it's expected that, along with HTML, you'll understand when to use Java, JavaScript, and/or Shockwave, and possibly even be able to do them all yourself. Learning the basics of Java will give you a leg up.

If you're a programmer, this applies even more to you. Java is by far the fastest growing segment of the field, and it isn't showing signs of slowing down. Adding Java to your resume will increase your opportunities.

Java skills are most important of all for freelancers and consultants. If you add Java to your list of skills, you're a much more attractive candidate to clients.

Common Java Myths

There are a number of common myths about what Java is, and what Java isn't. We'll set a few of them straight here.

Myth: Java is related to JavaScript

As described above, Java was designed at Sun Microsystems. JavaScript, on the other hand, was created by Netscape to be a client-side scripting addition to HTML, and was originally called LiveScript. When Java took off in a huge way, the smart folks at Netscape figured out how to get some of that buzz for themselves—by renaming LiveScript "JavaScript." It worked quite well from the hype standpoint, but has confused people ever since.

If you want to know more about JavaScript, I recommend looking at *JavaScript for the World Wide Web, Visual QuickStart Guide, 2nd Edition* by Tom Negrino and myself (Peachpit Press; 1998).

Myth: Java should be written JAVA

Java isn't an acronym, it's a word. Although I did once hear a claim that it "might" stand for "Just Another Vague Acronym"…

Myth: Java is just for the Web

In general, when people think of Java they think of little doodads running in browser windows over the Internet. And for the most part, that's the aspect of Java that most people are familiar with. The actual name for these doodads is *applets*. They're not stand-alone applications, in that they can't run by themselves and need a browser.

However, you can write perfectly acceptable applications with Java. Why would you want to? Well, because it's a small, simple, cross-platform language. And while this book is called *Java for the World Wide Web*, almost all of the concepts (except for those having to do with browsers, for example) also apply to stand-alone applications.

Figure 1.1 A DEC PDP-11. You won't be needing one of these.

Myth: Java is just on the client side

Some people who think that Java is just for the Web go further and think that Java is only on the client side; in other words, that it can only be run inside a browser. This couldn't be further from the truth.

One of the big growth areas for Java at the moment is in *servlets*. These, like applets, are mini-programs that run as part of another application, in this case, a Web server. And again, the reason for doing this is that Java is small, simple, and cross-platform. If you write one useful servlet, you can run it as part of UNIX, Windows, and Macintosh servers.

Myth: You have to learn another programming language first

For a programming language, Java is fairly easy to learn. There are a number of people who claim that you should learn C, or C++, or even Pascal first. I've found one thing in common with all of these people: They always recommend the language that *they* learned first.

Java is an excellent way to start learning object-oriented concepts, without a lot of the garbage that's in, for example, C++. If you learn Java first, you won't have to then unlearn all those bad habits. Consequently, this book doesn't make any comparisons like "For those of you who know SmallTalk, *this* is similar to *that*." For one thing, there are excellent books out there that will teach you Java when you already know another language; for another thing, all the SmallTalk programmers I know think that everyone should stop using Java and switch to SmallTalk instead.

Besides, if I recommended that you all learn programming the way I did, well, there's not a lot of PDP-11s running BASIC anymore . . . and I won't even talk about DEC-10 assembler on punchcards.

What you'll need

If you learned HTML or JavaScript, you probably didn't need to buy any new tools. A text editor was enough to get you started, with the possible later addition of a visual Web design tool. With Java, on the other hand, you're likely to need something more.

That something more is usually referred to as an *integrated development environment* (or IDE) or sometimes as a *compiler*. If you're on Windows 95/98/NT or Solaris, you might try your luck with the free utilities offered by Sun:

http://java.sun.com/products/jdk/1.0.2/tools/
→ win32/

http://java.sun.com/products/jdk/1.0.2/tools/
→ solaris/

While they are free, they're not exactly friendly to novices. If you want some hand-holding, or you're on a different platform, you'll want to check out Appendix A, which includes a list of some of the different development environments available.

✔ Tips

■ Given that there are so many different IDEs available, this book doesn't try to cover creating applets with each. The IDE you choose won't teach you Java, but it should tell you at least how to load it on your system and get started. And after that, you have this book.

■ If you're running Windows 95/98/NT or Solaris (as referenced above), an IDE isn't a requirement to use this book. You'll find life much, much easier with one, however.

Why this book covers Java 1.0

When I started writing this book at the beginning of 1998, everyone I talked to assumed that I was writing a Java 1.2 book. I'd say "No, I don't think that 1.2 is going to be ready that soon" (I turned out to be right on that, by the way), and they'd start to give me reasons why writing a Java 1.1 book was a mistake. When I'd say that I was writing a Java 1.0 book, they'd be speechless and stunned.

Why did I write a book on something that geeks consider to be so far behind the technology curve? Simple—because it works.

According to Netscape, as of this writing, none of the browsers they ship are, out of the box, completely compatible with Java 1.1 (see http://developer.netscape.com/docs/ → manuals/communicator/javajdk.html).

IE 4 does support version 1.1, but IE 3 only supports 1.0. So, what it comes down to is this: Do you want your Web pages to have bleeding-edge technology, or do you want them to work for the largest possible number of people? This book is geared toward people who are looking for the latter. (Of course, you'll also want to learn how things have changed in 1.1. That's covered in Appendix D.)

Don't get me wrong: If you're writing applications, or building an intranet where you have control over what browsers people are using, expecting people to have the latest and greatest is reasonable. But studies have shown that people are not upgrading their browsers as quickly as they used to, and if you care about making your pages accessible, you'll want to stick with 1.0 for the time being.

JAVA BASICS

One of the reasons that many people find computer programming intimidating is the large amount of jargon and buzzwords used by those "in the know." In this chapter, I'll explain commonly used Java jargon and concepts in plain English, with a minimum of Three Letter Acronyms (TLAs, for short).

Introducing the amazing Java Virtual Machine

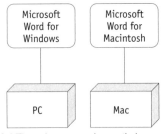

Figure 2.1 This is how normal compiled programs expect the world to look.

One of the most commonly used acronyms in Java is JVM, which stands for Java Virtual Machine. Understanding why the JVM exists is the key to understanding what's so special about Java.

Take a look at Figure 2.1, which shows how normal programs work. If you want to run MS Word on a PC, you need to buy the Wintel version. If you want to run it on a Mac, you need to buy the Mac version. If you buy the wrong version for your machine, your computer just won't be able to read what's on the disks. Programs that are machine-specific are said to be in *machine code*.

Java programs, on the other hand, look at the world differently, as shown in Figure 2.2. In order to run Java, your machine needs a piece of software called a Java Virtual Machine, or JVM. If you've ever run a Java applet or application on your computer, or if you have a modern browser, you've already got a JVM.

Java programs don't talk directly to your computer. Instead, they talk to the JVM, and the JVM talks to your computer. You can think of the JVM as a translator between the Java code and your computer, which is why Java code is referred to as *interpreted* code instead of *compiled* (machine-specific) code. The JVM is machine-specific code that runs on your computer. Its sole purpose in life is to take Java programs and convince your computer that they're really programs made to run on your particular machine.

As far as the Java program is concerned, the JVM might as well be the computer itself, since that's as close to the hardware as it gets. That's why it's called a "virtual machine."

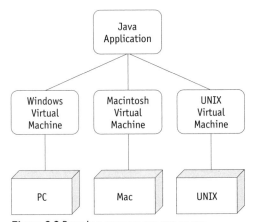

Figure 2.2 But a Java program can run on any hardware, so long as there's a Java Virtual Machine running on it.

Java Security

One of the main reasons for Java's popularity is that it's secure. This means that someone cannot write a Java applet which, when run through your browser, will delete files from your hard drive or e-mail your credit card numbers.

Java manages this using the concept of the *sandbox*. When Java applets are restricted to playing in the sandbox, there's a long list of things that they can't do on a browser's machine. Java applets cannot read, write, delete, rename, or check for the existence of files. They cannot list or create directories, nor can they check to see if a given file name is a file or directory. They also cannot print or create a network connection to a computer other than the one from which the code itself was loaded.

This changes, to some degree, in later versions of Java (see Appendix D for more information).

Java files

When you start writing a Java program, you'll begin by creating an AppletName.java file in your development environment. This file, with the name ending in ".java," will contain the source code that you type in, as shown in Figure 2.3.

When you compile your program, a new file will be created, one that ends with ".class." This file is the one that's understood by the JVM. It contains something called *bytecodes*, which are the result of the compilation of your program and serve as the input to the JVM. Figure 2.4 looks like garbage to us, but it's everything the JVM needs to know.

When you upload your applet to your server, you only need to upload the .class file. It may seem odd that you don't need to upload the file that you actually worked on, but you don't have to (unless you want the world to see your source code!).

Figure 2.3 Here's what the code for HelloWorld.java looks like.

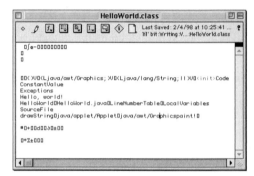

Figure 2.4 And here's what HelloWorld.class looks like; HelloWorld.java has been translated into bytecodes that the JVM can understand.

Figure 2.5 This cat object's name is Pixel. His Web site is at http://www.chalcedony.com/pixel.

Figure 2.6 This gone-but-not-forgotten cat object's name was Mutant Alien From Hell... really, it was.

Buzzword Bingo

The following sections will help you to understand some Java-related terms that we will use throughout this book.

Object

Close your eyes and picture a cat in your mind. Think about four legs, paws, and fur. That abstract idea in your head is a cat object. Unless (like me at this moment) you have a cat sitting in your lap right now, it's a completely abstract object; in other words, that cat doesn't actually exist. That's okay, it's still a cat object.

To know what objects Java has that you can play with, check out < http://java.sun.com/ → docs/api_documentation.html>. It contains documentation for all the objects that come with Java. If you need any other objects, you'll have to create them yourself. Luckily, that's not too difficult.

Instance

In order for you to pet that cat you're thinking of, it's got to be an actual cat. In Java, this is referred to as an *instance* of an object. The object itself is an abstract idea. In order for it to exist, you have to create an instance. You can have multiple instances of an object; Figures 2.5 and 2.6 show two instances of the cat object. You'll learn how to create instances of objects in your code starting in Chapter 4.

For example, say you want to build a desk. You know just what you want the desk to look like, so you draw a picture on a piece of paper as a blueprint. That picture is an object: it's not a desk, but it can be used to create a desk. You can then create several identical desks, all from that one blueprint. You can give the blueprint to a friend, and they can create a desk (or several desks) just like yours.

Copies can be made of your blueprint, and people all over the world can create more desks. The desks that are built are instances of that desk object that you designed when you drew the picture.

Java, for example, contains a Font object. In order to create a font that you can work with, you need to create an instance of the Font object. This is done by adding a line to your applet:

```
Font f = new Font("TimesRoman",Font.BOLD,24);
```

This creates a new instance (named f) of the Font object. That new font is then set to the font of 24 point Times Roman Bold.

Instantiate

This is one of the ugliest, most confusing words in Java, and all it means is "create an instance of." If you instantiate a cat object, in English, it just means that you create another cat. If you instantiate a desk, it means that you got out the hammer, nails, and lumber, and built another real-world desk.

Instantiation/Instantiating

These are just more ways of referring to the process of creating an instance.

Method

The things that objects can do are called *methods*. It might be helpful for you to think of objects as nouns and methods as verbs. For instance, you could check to see if a cat object isPurring(). Note the parentheses; they indicate that you're referring to a method.

Dot Syntax

Now that we have these objects and methods, how are they put together? Java uses something called dot syntax, which JavaScript users should find familiar.

What's Buzzword Bingo?

Buzzword Bingo is a game popularized by Scott Adams' comic strip "Dilbert." You and your coworkers each take 24 examples of commonly used jargon and put them onto a card with a Bingo game grid. Then you take the card into a meeting with management and check off a square every time someone uses the phrase. Whoever fills up a row, column, or diagonal on their card first wins.

Many Java books read like someone trying to force a quick end to a game of Buzzword Bingo.

For more about Buzzword Bingo, check out http://www.buzzword-bingo.com. As of this writing, their top ten buzzwords are Branding, Portal Site, Proactive, Y2K, Merger, Acquisition, Affiliate Programs, Outside the Box, Robust, and Turnkey Solution.

You can put together objects and their methods by simplying separating them with periods (or dots). This is called *dot syntax*. Here's some examples:

cat.isPurring()

desk.hasReturn()

Font.getSize()

Instance Variables

Objects have instance variables. For that cat object, the instance variable numberOfLegs is four. Note that instance variables are different from methods: There's no parentheses, because no action is taking place.

Instance variables describe something about the object. For example:

◆ cat.numberOfLegs contains how many legs this cat has.

◆ desk.typeOfWood contains what material the desk is made of.

◆ Rectangle.height is an actual Java instance variable that contains the height of a rectangle object.

Objects consist of other objects

Java starts with little tiny objects, and puts them together to create big, complex objects. This means that if you have something complex, you can break it down into simple components. Take desk.typeOfWood from our previous example. That object would be just a short piece of text, which Java calls a *string*. Strings are objects in their own right, with their own methods, such as length(). So, you could refer to desk.typeOfWood.length() to get the length of the name of the type of wood that the desk is made out of.

An example from Java is userCheckbox.get → Current().getLabel(). In this example there are a group of checkboxes (called userCheckbox), which have been set up to be radio buttons.

To find out which radio button is currently selected, we look at userCheckbox.getCurrent(). That just returns a checkbox to us, not a name, so we need to look at the check box's label. Calling the getLabel() method on userCheckbox. → getCurrent() gives us the value we need.

Class

If you combine an object with all its associated instance variables and all its associated methods, you have a *class*. So far, we've discussed the cat object. If you take everything you know about the cat object, along with its associated instance variables (numberOfLegs, eyeColor, noseColor, furLength) and its associated methods (isPurring(), wetNose(), isEating(), isSleeping()), you'll have the class Cat. When you create a cat object, you're creating an instance of the Cat class, and all of its associated instance variables and methods are available to your code.

If you created the cat object and it's methods, you know what the cat class contains. Otherwise, you'll need to refer to documentation, based on what the cat class extends (see below).

An actual Java example is a Rectangle, which has instance variables x and y (designating the starting points), as well as height and width, and methods such as isEmpty().

Font is another class, which contains the methods getFont(), getSize(), and getStyle().

Constructors

Constructors are another part of a class; you call them to create an object. You could create a new cat object by calling Cat("Pixel"). You can create a new font object by calling Font → ("Helvetica",Font.ITALIC,36).

Alternatively, you could create a new Rectangle either by calling Rectangle(x, y, width, height), or by calling Rectangle(point, dimension).

A class can have several different constructors, i.e., several different ways to create the same object.

A group of checkboxes could be created by calling:

```
new Checkbox("Breakfast");
new Checkbox("Lunch");
new Checkbox("Dinner");
```

or by calling:

```
new Checkbox("Breakfast",true);
new Checkbox("Lunch",false);
new Checkbox("Dinner",false);
```

The former uses the default value (not checked) for whether the checkbox is checked or not, the latter style explicitly sets whether the checkbox is checked or not.

Inheritance

Java derives a great deal of its power from the concept of inheritance. For instance, you may have a class HousePet, which includes the methods isEating() and isSleeping(). Then you can create the classes Cat and Dog, having them inherit everything that's in HousePet, including those two methods.

Extends

When one class gets its characteristics from another through inheritance, it is said to *extend* that class. Cat extends the class HousePet, so Cat can also be referred to, then, as a *subclass* of HousePet.

In Java, for example, Dialog extends Window. This means that a dialog box is a specific type of a window. Dialog inherits everything that Window contains, but a few methods are then added to Dialog that apply only to dialog boxes.

In this book, we'll be writing applets, so everything we do will be extending the Java class **java.applet**. Consequently, our applets will inherit everything that Java provides Applet, as a starting point for everything that we write.

Package

A group of related classes is called a package.

AWT

AWT stands for Abstract Windowing Toolkit. The AWT package is used to display information in a window, which means that we'll be seeing a lot of it in this book.

JDK

JDK stands for Java Development Kit. Each version of the JDK is associated with a version of Java; for example, Java 1.0 is also referred to as JDK 1.0.

BUZZWORD BINGO

USING JAVA
ON YOUR PAGES

You don't actually have to know Java to put Java applets on your pages. You can get applets from any number of places, and just use the HTML **APPLET** tag to place them where you want them. In this chapter, we'll look at where to get applets over the Internet (often for free) and how to place them on your pages.

Placing Java applets on your pages

Surprisingly, you can make extensive use of Java applets on your Web pages without ever learning the Java language. Listing 3.1 is an example of an HTML file that uses the APPLET tag to add an applet to the Web page.

To place a Java applet on your Web page:

1. <APPLET CODEBASE="classes" CODE=
→ "HelloWorld.class" WIDTH=200 HEIGHT=50>

The APPLET tag is a standard part of HTML. The attributes we're using here are CODEBASE (the directory where the applet resides on the server), CODE (the name of the applet's class file), and HEIGHT and WIDTH (which tell the browser how much room the Java applet will take up on the page).

In this case, we're calling the HelloWorld applet. The class file (described in chapter 2) is named HelloWorld.class, and it resides in the classes directory. The width is 200 and the height is 50. Figure 3.1 shows what the applet looks like on a Web page.

2. </APPLET>

This ends the APPLET tag.

✔ Tip

■ If you have applets that are shared by multiple pages on your site, use the CODEBASE attribute of the APPLET tag to refer to the applet in a common directory. That way, if you change the applet later, you won't have to touch the HTML files.

Listing 3.1 It's really pretty straightforward to add a Java applet to your Web page.

```
<HTML>
<HEAD>
 <TITLE>Hey, it's Java</TITLE>
</HEAD>
<BODY BGCOLOR=WHITE>
 <APPLET CODEBASE="classes"
 →CODE="HelloWorld.class" WIDTH=200 HEIGHT=50>
 </APPLET>
</BODY>
</HTML>
```

Figure 3.1 This is what the HelloWorld applet looks like on a Web page.

Listing 3.2 Always be sure to display a message for non-Java-enabled browsers.

```
<HTML>
<HEAD>
 <TITLE>Hey, it's Java</TITLE>
</HEAD>
<BODY BGCOLOR=WHITE>
 <APPLET CODEBASE="classes" CODE=
 → "HelloWorld.class" WIDTH=200 HEIGHT=50>
 <H1>If you had Java, you'd be seeing a cool
 → applet now</H1>
 </APPLET>
</BODY>
</HTML>
```

Figure 3.2 Let people know that they should upgrade and find out what they're missing.

Figure 3.3 If you don't have Java enabled, you can't see the cool Java effects.

To enable Java in your browser:

Some browsers, such as Netscape 4, allow Java to be disabled. If Java has been disabled in your browser, you'll want to enable it so you can see Java in action. Figure 3.3 shows Netscape's Advanced preferences, which include a checkbox to enable or disable Java.

Displaying a message for non-Java browsers

While most browsers these days have Java, some people use old browsers, and some surf the Web with Java turned off. In these cases, you should display a message letting people know what cool thing they're missing, as demonstrated in Listing 3.2.

To display a message for browsers without Java:

1. <H1>If you had Java, you'd be seeing a cool → applet now</H1>

   You might think that this looks just like normal HTML, and you'd be correct— it is. However, because it's within the APPLET tag, it's only shown when the user can't display the Java applet. Figure 3.2 shows how this displays on the screen.

✔ Tips

- In Figure 3.2, you might notice that the "no Java" message isn't in the same area that's set aside for the Java applet. Because the browser doesn't understand Java, it doesn't know about the HEIGHT and WIDTH attributes in the APPLET tag. Be sure to keep this in mind when laying out your pages.

- Any HTML tags can go into this area. Be creative, but also be careful about closing any tags you open.

Positioning Java applets on the page

The APPLET tag can be positioned on a Web page much like the IMG tag. Listings 3.3 and 3.4 show how an applet can be moved from the default alignment.

To position a Java applet:

1. <APPLET CODEBASE="classes" CODE=
→ "HelloWorld.class" WIDTH=200 HEIGHT=50
→ ALIGN=RIGHT>

In Figure 3.4, the HelloWorld applet is on the right side of the window. This is because the ALIGN attribute of the APPLET tag has been set to RIGHT.

2. <APPLET CODEBASE="classes" CODE=
→ "HelloWorld.class" WIDTH=200 HEIGHT=50
→ HSPACE=100 VSPACE=100>

In Figure 3.5, the HelloWorld applet is surrounded by 100 pixels of white space on all sides, due to the settings of the HSPACE and VSPACE attributes.

Listing 3.3 Here's a way to move an applet from its default position.

```
<HTML>
<HEAD>
  <TITLE>Hey, it's Java</TITLE>
</HEAD>
<BODY BGCOLOR=WHITE>
  <APPLET CODEBASE="classes"
  → CODE="HelloWorld.class" WIDTH=200 HEIGHT=50
  → ALIGN=RIGHT>
  </APPLET>
</BODY>
</HTML>
```

Figure 3.4 Here the applet is aligned on the right-hand side of the window.

Listing 3.4 Here's another way to move an applet around.

```
<HTML>
<HEAD>
  <TITLE>Hey, it's Java</TITLE>
</HEAD>
<BODY BGCOLOR=WHITE>
  <APPLET CODEBASE="classes"
  → CODE="HelloWorld.class" WIDTH=200 HEIGHT=50
  → HSPACE=100 VSPACE=100>
  </APPLET>
</BODY>
</HTML>
```

Figure 3.5 The applet now has a 100-pixel-wide border on every side.

✔ Tips

- Other valid values for ALIGN are LEFT, RIGHT, TOP, TEXTTOP, MIDDLE, ABSMIDDLE, BASELINE, BOTTOM, and ABSBOTTOM, as described in Table 3.1.

- HEIGHT, WIDTH, ALIGN, HSPACE, and VSPACE are all attributes that the APPLET tag shares with the IMG tag. To learn more about these attributes, check out *HTML 4 for the World Wide Web*, by Elizabeth Castro. (Peachpit Press, 1998)

Table 3.1

Alignment Values	
ALIGNMENT	**MEANING**
LEFT	Aligns the applet area flush left
RIGHT	Aligns the applet area flush right
TOP	Displays the applet area at the top of the available area
TEXTTOP	Aligns the applet area with the highest text displayed adjacent to the applet area
MIDDLE	Aligns the middle of the applet area with the baseline of adjacent text
ABSMIDDLE	Aligns the middle of the applet area with the middle of the largest adjacent item
BASELINE	Aligns the bottom of the applet area with the baseline of adjacent text
BOTTOM	Aligns the bottom of the applet area with the bottom of adjacent text
ABSBOTTOM	Aligns the bottom of the applet area with the bottom of largest adjacent item

POSITIONING JAVA APPLETS ON THE PAGE

Finding applets on the Internet

There are a number of resources on the Internet that can provide you with free or inexpensive applets. One of the oldest and best-known is the Gamelan archive, at http://www.gamelan.com. Before you go to the trouble of writing your own applet, it doesn't hurt to see if someone has already invented that particular wheel.

In this case, we're going to look for a news scroller applet, similar to the ones used by CNN and MSNBC.

To get an applet off the Internet:

1. Figure 3.6 shows the Gamelan home page. In this case, we're going to check out "Special Effects," which as of today has 1129 entries.

2. Figure 3.7 shows all the different types of special effects currently available through this resource. For a scroller applet, we'll look in "Text Utilities," with its 426 entries.

3. In the "Java: Special Effects: Text Utilities" area, as shown in Figure 3.8, there's a listing for 177 different scrolling text applets.

4. One of the first applets on the list (as shown in Figure 3.9) is tinyScroller, which sounds like it'll do the trick. Clicking on the name of the applet takes us to the page that the author of the applet has set up to describe it, at http://www.
→ diac.com/~cricci/java.html.

Figure 3.6 The Gamelan Directory has thousands of different entries about Java.

Figure 3.7 There are over 1000 different special-effects applets...

Figure 3.8 ...including hundreds of different text utilities.

Figure 3.9 There are almost 200 different applets just for scrolling text.

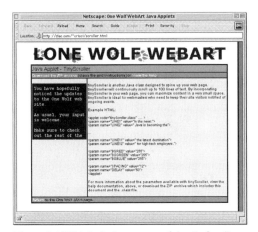

Figure 3.10 This is the home page of the tinyScroller applet.

5. At this page, as shown in Figure 3.10, we find the two things we need: the class file and documentation of how the applet works. Since tinyScroller is freeware, this is all we need.

✔ Tip

■ There are numerous other places on the Internet where you can find applets, some of which are listed in Appendix A.

Passing parameters to an applet

In order to use a canned applet, you need a way to pass parameters from HTML to Java. In other words, someone who knows only HTML should be able to get the applet to display something different by making changes to the page in HTML. This is accomplished by means of the PARAM tag used within the APPLET tag as shown in Listing 3.5.

A well-documented applet will include a list of all the possible parameters, showing all the possible values including default values. The documentation for the tinyScroller applet (as downloaded in the previous section) is shown in the sidebar on the next page.

If a canned applet doesn't accept parameters you can still use it on your page, but it means that what you're displaying isn't personalized in any way—anyone else with the same applet will have identical results. Here, we pass parameters to the tinyScroller applet to display a unique page.

Listing 3.5. This example shows how to refer to an applet with multiple parameters.

```
<HTML>
<HEAD>
 <TITLE>Tiny Scroller</TITLE>
</HEAD>
<BODY BGCOLOR=WHITE>
 <APPLET CODEBASE="classes" CODE=
 →"tinyScroller.class" WIDTH=200 HEIGHT=150>
  <PARAM NAME="LINE1" VALUE="In today's top
  → story:">
  <PARAM NAME="LINE2" VALUE=" Java: Visual
  → QuickStart Guide">
  <PARAM NAME="LINE3" VALUE=" breaks all
  → previous sales">
  <PARAM NAME="LINE4" VALUE=" records, as rumor
  → spreads">
  <PARAM NAME="LINE5" VALUE=" that book
  → contains">
  <PARAM NAME="LINE6" VALUE=" hard-hitting
  → information,">
  <PARAM NAME="LINE7" VALUE=" sparkling prose,">
  <PARAM NAME="LINE8" VALUE=" live nude girls,">
  <PARAM NAME="LINE9" VALUE=" and free beer">
  <PARAM NAME="BGRED" VALUE="255">
  <PARAM NAME="BGGREEN" VALUE="255">
  <PARAM NAME="BGBLUE" VALUE="255">
  <PARAM NAME="FGRED" VALUE="0">
  <PARAM NAME="FGGREEN" VALUE="0">
  <PARAM NAME="FGBLUE" VALUE="0">
  <PARAM NAME="DELAY" VALUE="5">
  <PARAM NAME="MAXLINE" VALUE="9">
  <H1>You should use a Java-enabled
  → browser!</H1>
 </APPLET>
</BODY>
</HTML>
```

The tinyScroller applet

The documentation for the **tinyScroller** applet reads:

tinyScroller v0.81 (Java Class)

tinyScroller is another Java class designed to spice up your Web page. **tinyScroller** will continuously scroll up to 12 lines of text. By incorporating **tinyScroller** in your Web page, you can maximize content in a very small space. **tinyScroller** is ideal for Webmasters who need to keep their site visitors notified of ongoing events.

tinyScroller, like **tinyFader**, is extremely customizable. I've made many of the attributes settable as parameters passed from your HTML. Below, you'll find documented all of the current parameters.

Example HTML:

```
<applet code="tinyScroller.class" height="150" width="175">
<param name="LINE1" value="In the news:">
<param name="LINE2" value=" Java is becoming the">
...
<param name="LINE11" value=" the latest destination">
<param name="LINE12" value=" for high-tech employers.">
<param name="BGRED" value="255">
<param name="BGGREEN" value="255">
<param name="BGBLUE" value="255">
<param name="SPACING" value="12">
<param name="DELAY" value="50">
<param name="MAXLINE" value="12">
</applet>
```

Parameters

LINE1–LINE12 (Required) - LINE1 through LINE12 make up the content to be displayed. If you're not using all 12 lines you don't have to define them, but rember to correctly set the MAXLINE parameter.

MAXLINE (Optional) - If you are not using all 12 lines available, make sure to correctly set MAXLINE to the actual number of lines used. I'm suppressing errors so if you choose to scroll more lines than you actually defined you can do so by resetting this value. MAXLINE defaults to 12.

BGRED, BGGREEN, BGBLUE (Optional) - You may set the background color of the applet by passing the one-byte (0-255) RGB (red, green, and blue) component values. The background color defaults to white.

FGRED, FGGREEN, FGBLUE (Optional) - You may set the foreground (font) color for the applet by passing the one-byte (0-255) RGB (red, green, and blue) component values. The foreground color defaults to white.

SPACING (Optional) - You may define the line spacing by passing it as a parameter. SPACING defaults to 12.

DELAY (Optional) - DELAY controls the time interval between shifts in the line positions. Delay defaults to 100 milliseconds.

XPOS (Optional) - XPOS stands for X position; this controls the horizontal position of the lines within the applet. XPOS defaults to five.

BACKGROUND (Optional) - If you wish to use a graphic for the background of the applet, pass the filename here. You may pass a JPG or GIF. Displaying a graphic does, however, impact the speed of the screen update. As a result, you may notice a flicker.

The **tinyScroller** applet is © Christian Ricci, who may be reached at cricci@diac.com. The **tinyScroller** page is http://www.diac.com/~cricci/scroller.html.

To pass parameters to an applet:

1. `<PARAM NAME="LINE1" VALUE="In today's`
→ `top story:">`
`<PARAM NAME="LINE2" VALUE=" Java:Visual`
→ `QuickStart Guide">`

A PARAM tag consists of two attributes, NAME and VALUE, both of which are required. For each NAME, there must be an associated VALUE. For this use of the tinyScroller applet, we'll set LINE1 through LINE9 to get the results that we see scrolled in Figures 3.11 and 3.12.

2. `<PARAM NAME="BGRED" VALUE="255">`
`<PARAM NAME="BGGREEN" VALUE="255">`
`<PARAM NAME="BGBLUE" VALUE="255">`
`<PARAM NAME="FGRED" VALUE="0">`
`<PARAM NAME="FGGREEN" VALUE="0">`
`<PARAM NAME="FGBLUE" VALUE="0">`

Here we set the background color to white (red, green, and blue all set to 255) and the foreground color to black (red, green, and blue all set to 0). These are the defaults, so the Web page display would be the same even if these values were missing.

3. `<PARAM NAME="DELAY" VALUE="5">`
`<PARAM NAME="MAXLINE" VALUE="9">`

The default value of DELAY is 100 milliseconds, but that seems somewhat slow, so we reset it here to 5 milliseconds. If there are less than 12 lines to scroll, MAXLINE needs to be set to the correct number, which in this case is 9.

✔ Tip

■ In the above example, the parameters for BACKGROUND, XPOS, and SPACING were not set, as the defaults were acceptable. The background and foreground colors could also have been left off, as they're just using the defaults.

Figure 3.11 The text comes up from the bottom...

Figure 3.12 ...and scrolls off at the top.

PASSING PARAMETERS TO AN APPLET

YOUR FIRST APPLETS

By now you may be saying, "Hey, when do we get to start writing our own applets, already? This is supposed to be a book on writing Java, not just how to use existing programs!"

In this chapter we'll start getting into the code—we'll start off slow, then add pieces one at a time.

"Hello, World"

It's a tradition that the first program you write in a language always prints out the phrase "Hello, World." I don't know why, but it's required. In Applet 4.1, you see how it's done; Listing 4.1 shows the HTML file; and Figure 4.1 shows your message to the world in a Web browser.

To write your first applet:

1. public class HelloWorld extends java.applet.
   → Applet

   This starts off your applet. What you're writing is a new class, one that extends the standard Applet class. The name of this new class is HelloWorld.

   Public, here and everywhere else, means that we're not worried about who's accessing this applet.

2. {

   The left curly bracket is used to show that the following statements are within the class we've just started.

3. public void paint(java.awt.Graphics g)

   Paint() is a method of HelloWorld. We want to display something on the screen, so we're going to have paint() do the work for us.

   The paint() method is declared void, because it doesn't return anything. Later we'll see methods that return a value.

   Paint()is passed (referring to the value within the parenthesis) a Graphics object. Within paint(), we want to give that object a shorter name than java.awt.Graphics, so we'll call it g.

4. {

   The left curly bracket shows that any following statements are inside this method.

Applet 4.1 This applet displays the infamous "Hello, World" message that tradition requires all new programmers to write.

```
 Applet
public class HelloWorld extends
→ java.applet.Applet {

  public void paint(java.awt.Graphics g) {
    g.drawString("Hello, world!", 100 , 25);
  }

}
```

Listing 4.1 This HTML file calls the HelloWorld.class file within an applet tag.

```
 Listing
<HTML>
<HEAD>
 <TITLE>My First Applet</TITLE>
</HEAD>
<BODY BGCOLOR=WHITE>
 <APPLET CODEBASE="Java Classes"
 → CODE="HelloWorld.class" WIDTH=400 HEIGHT=50>
 </APPLET>
</BODY>
</HTML>
```

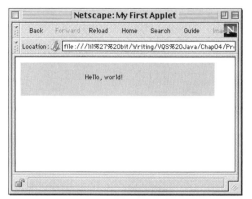

Figure 4.1 Congratulations, you've passed your initiation and written your first Java applet!

5. g.drawString("Hello, world!", 100 , 25);

Now, we use g (that graphics object we named in the previous step) to draw a string in the browser window. We're going to draw it at 100 pixels over and 25 pixels down, and the text we're printing is "Hello, world!"

6. }

The right curly bracket signifies the end of the paint method.

7. }

This finishes off the HelloWorld class.

✔ Tip

- If you're used to JavaScript, you might be wondering whether the semicolon at the end of step 5 is necessary. This is another of the many differences between Java and JavaScript—in JavaScript, they're optional, but in Java, they're required.

"HELLO, WORLD"

Using fonts

Being able to write out "Hello, World" is pretty cool, until you realize that you could do that perfectly well within HTML. One of the simplest things you can do in Java that you can't do in HTML is use explicit fonts and point sizes. Applet 4.2 shows the same applet, but this time with the phrase written in 36-point bold Times Roman (as shown in Figure 4.2).

To specify fonts in an applet:

1. import java.awt.Graphics;
   import java.awt.Font;

   Rather than always refer to java.awt. → Graphics by its full name (which is rather long, isn't it?) we can tell Java to just import the entire class. Once that's done, a simple reference to Graphics is sufficient. In these two lines, both Graphics and Font are imported.

2. Font f = new Font("TimesRoman",Font.BOLD, → 36);

   This line creates a new font object named f, and sets it to be initialized to 36-point bold Times Roman.

3. g.setFont(f);

   Within the paint method, we set the graphic object g to use the value of the font object f we set in the previous step.

✔ Tip

■ Java fonts aren't what you'd expect to find on your system, as Java has its own fonts, which have no relationship to the ones that you're used to using on your computer. In Java, you can expect to find Courier, Dialog, Helvetica, TimesRoman, and Symbol. Table 4.1 shows how each of these will display on your system.

Applet 4.2 Now, we say it big and bold.

```
import java.awt.Graphics;
import java.awt.Font;

public class HelloWorld extends
→ java.applet.Applet {

  Font f = new Font("TimesRoman",Font.BOLD,36);

  public void paint(Graphics g) {
    g.setFont(f);
    g.drawString("Hello, world!", 100 , 25);
  }

}
```

Figure 4.2 That's a little more friendly!

Table 4.1

Java Font Mapping		
JAVA FONTS	**MAC FONTS**	**WINDOWS FONTS**
Courier	Courier	Courier New
Dialog	Geneva	MS Sans Serif
Helvetica	Helvetica	Arial
Symbol	Symbol	WingDings
TimesRoman	Times Roman	Times New Roman

Applet 4.3 Use the init method to set the applet's background

```
                     Applet

import java.awt.*;

public class HelloWorld extends
→ java.applet.Applet {

  Font f = new Font("TimesRoman",Font.BOLD,36);

  public void init() {
    setBackground(Color.white);
  }

  public void paint(Graphics g) {
    g.setFont(f);
    g.drawString("Hello, world!", 100 , 25);
  }

}
```

Hello, world!

Figure 4.3 Now we look less like newbie applet writers.

Setting the background color

Even though we now have our text just the way we want it, we're still displaying on that ugly, plain default shade of gray. There's a way to change that, too, to make the applet blend in with the rest of the HTML page. Figure 4.3 shows the much more pleasant appearance of Applet 4.3.

To change the background color:

1. public void init() {

This is a new method, init(). This method is useful for things that you want to set the first time and never again.

2. setBackground(Color.white);

The setBackground command sets the background for the applet on the HTML page. In this case, we're setting the background color to white.

3. }

The right curly bracket ends the init() method.

✔ Tips

■ The colors that can be used by name (such as white, above) are black, blue, cyan, darkGray, gray, green, lightGray, magenta, orange, pink, red, white, and yellow.

■ Other colors can be used by calculating the hexidecimal value of the color, just as in HTML. In this case, you would say setBackground(new Color(Integer.valueOf
→ ("#2B2B2B")))

■ We've changed the beginning import value again, this time to java.awt.*. This says that, instead of importing just one or two parts of java.awt, we'll just import everything at once.

Passing parameters from HTML to Java

In a previous chapter, we saw how to pass information from HTML to Java. Applet 4.4 shows how you can write an applet so that it reads information from an HTML file. Figure 4.4 shows the results of this applet when run with the HTML file shown in Listing 4.2.

To read parameters from HTML:

1. String whatToSay;

   This line declares a new string variable, whatToSay. This will contain the text that we want to print in the browser window.

2. this.whatToSay =
   → getParameter("whatToSay");

   The HTML file contains a <PARAM> tag within the <APPLET> tag. This param tag has two attributes: NAME and VALUE. In the applet, getParameter() reads the value passed in for that particular named param tag. In this case, the name of the parameter is whatToSay, and the value of the string is set to "Hello, readers!"

3. if (this.whatToSay == null) {

   Just in case we didn't find a valid parameter, we should set the string value to something. To check its status, we compare it to null. If they're equal, we need to give it a value.

4. this.whatToSay = "Hello, world!";

   How about the traditional "Hello, world!," just to let us know that we didn't pass in something more edifying?

5. }

   The right curly bracket closes off the if statement.

Listing 4.2 We use HTML to pass the phrase "Hello, readers!" to our Java applet.

```
<HTML>
<HEAD>
 <TITLE>My First Applet</TITLE>
</HEAD>
<BODY BGCOLOR=WHITE>
 <APPLET CODEBASE="Java Classes" CODE="Hello
 →World.class" WIDTH=400 HEIGHT=50>
 <PARAM NAME=whatToSay VALUE="Hello, readers!">
 </APPLET>
</BODY>
</HTML>
```

Applet 4.4 We grab the passed parameter from HTML in the init method.

```
import java.awt.*;

public class HelloWorld extends
→ java.applet.Applet {
 Font f = new Font("TimesRoman",Font.BOLD,36);
 String whatToSay;

 public void init() {
   setBackground(Color.white);
   this.whatToSay = getParameter("whatToSay");
   if (this.whatToSay == null) {
     this.whatToSay = "Hello, world!";
   }
 }

 public void paint(Graphics g) {
   g.setFont(f);
   g.drawString(this.whatToSay, 100 , 25);
 }

}
```

Figure 4.4 And then, the applet shows the result.

The Seven Common Methods

There are seven methods that are commonly used in applets. This is referred to as "overriding," because they already exist for applets—if you use them, you're overriding the default. If you use one of these methods, that method is said to be "overriden." The seven are:

◆ init(): Use this when you want something to happen when the applet is initialized.

◆ start(): This is called when the applet becomes visible, after init has completed or when an applet.

◆ stop(): Called when the applet is no longer displayed, such as when the page is closed, or hidden.

◆ destroy(): The last step before an applet is closed; this is the cleaning-up step.

The previous four are all part of java.applet.Applet. The next three are part of java.awt.Component.

◆ paint(): Displays the applet.

◆ repaint(): Tells Java to call update as soon as possible.

◆ update(): Redraws the applet by calling paint.

✔ Tip

■ Where did that this come from, and what does it mean? The variable whatToSay has been defined as part of the class. When the method inside that same class refers to whatToSay, the method needs to know that it's a local variable. The Java keyword this is used to make that clear. You can think of this as meaning "Which whatToSay are we referring to here? Oh, the one that's part of this class; this one." Whenever this is used, it means we're referring to a variable that the method should know about from within the class.

Adding comments

All good programmers add comments to their programs. The sooner you get into the habit, the easier you'll find learning Java, especially when you need to refer back to your code later. Applet 4.5 shows the same applet as in the previous example, with the addition of two comments.

To add comments:

1. /*
   This is my first applet
   */

There are two kinds of comments in Java, single-line and multi-line. This is a multi-line comment. It starts with the "/*" (slash and asterisk) characters, and Java ignores everything until it finds a following "*/" (asterisk then slash). It's an excellent idea to get in the habit of always starting your program with a comment stating what the code does.

2. // The string whatToSay is passed from
   → JavaScript

This is a single-line comment. It can be anywhere in a line, either at the beginning of the line or following some code. In either case, everything to the right of the two slashes is a comment. The comment area ends at the line break.

Applet 4.5 Always comment your code—you'll be happy you did later!

```
/*
  This is my first applet
*/
import java.awt.*;

public class HelloWorld extends java.applet.
 Applet {
 Font f = new Font("TimesRoman",Font.BOLD,36);
 String whatToSay;

 public void init() {
   setBackground(Color.white);
   this.whatToSay = getParameter("whatToSay");
   //The value above is passed from HTML
   if (this.whatToSay == null) {
     this.whatToSay = "Hello, world!";
   }
 }

 public void paint(Graphics g) {
   g.setFont(f);
   g.drawString(this.whatToSay, 100 , 25);
 }

}
```

Applet 4.6 An example of using other font styles.

```
                    Applet
/*
 This is my first applet
 Here we show how to change the font style
*/
import java.applet.*;
import java.awt.*;

public class HelloWorld extends Applet {
  Font f = new Font("TimesRoman",Font.ITALIC,36);

  public void init() {
    setBackground(Color.white);
  }

  public void paint(Graphics g) {
    g.setFont(f);
    g.drawString("Now in Italics", 100 , 25);
  }

}
```

Figure 4.5 And here's what it looks like in your applet.

Changing the font style

Bold text is OK, but you don't want it all the time. Applet 4.6 changes the font style as shown in Figure 4.5.

To change font styles:

◆ Font f = new Font("TimesRoman",Font.ITALIC,
  → 36);

  Instead of Font.BOLD, use Font.ITALIC to display the text in italic 36-point Times Roman.

✔ Tips

■ The font styles understood by Java are Font.PLAIN, Font.BOLD, and Font.ITALIC.
  Each of these styles is really just stored as a number. So when you want a string to be both bold and italic, simply add the two together: Font.BOLD + Font.ITALIC.

Changing colors

Along with font faces, sizes, and styles, Java gives you control over colors. Figure 4.6 shows the results of Applet 4.7, which changes the font color to red.

To change colors:

◆ g.setColor(Color.red);

Just before we call g.drawString() to display the message, we call g.setColor() to change the color of the graphics object g. In this case, we set the color of the message to red.

✔ Tip

■ The colors available here are the same colors listed in *Setting the background color*, in this chapter.

Applet 4.7 You can use Java to display colored text.

```
/*
  This is my first applet
  Here we show how to change the font color
*/
import java.applet.*;
import java.awt.*;

public class HelloWorld extends Applet {
  Font f = new Font("TimesRoman",Font.BOLD,36);

  public void init() {
    setBackground(Color.white);
  }

  public void paint(Graphics g) {
    g.setFont(f);
    g.setColor(Color.red);
    g.drawString("Wow—Red!", 100 , 25);
  }

}
```

Figure 4.6 Here's an example of bright red text.

STRINGS AND THINGS

In the last chapter, we used some variables without really understanding what they were. Here, we'll cover the concept in depth.

Java and other programming languages use variables to store information so you can refer to it again later in your program. For example, we can set the variable myName to "Dori." In Java, this is written as myName = Dori. The equal sign means "is set to." Afterwards, the variable myName can be used anytime we need the value "Dori."

If someone else uses this applet later, they can set myName to "Sean" by simply replacing the previous statement with myName = Sean in the applet. Anywhere the code later references the myName variable, it will automatically see the name "Sean" instead of the name "Dori."

String variables

One of the basic types of variable you'll need is the string variable. A *string* is any piece of text between two quote symbols. Listing 5.1 and Applet 5.1 show our first example of a string variable.

To declare and use a string variable:

1. String stringVarWithValue = "Hey, I'm a
   → string!";

   This line creates a new string variable, called stringVarWithValue. At the same time we create it, we give it a value of "Hey, I'm a string!".

2. g.drawString(this.stringVarWithValue, 50 ,
   → 150);

   This line draws the string this.stringVarWithValue at the position 50 pixels over and 150 pixels down as shown in Figure 5.1.

✔ Tips

- Note that when we want to display something in the applet area, we put the code in the paint() method.

- A variable can be named almost anything, with just a few limitations. The name must start with a letter, dollar sign ($) or underscore (_), and after that may contain any number or letter. This means, for example, that variable names cannot contains spaces or dashes.

Listing 5.1 This HTML file calls Applet 5.1.

```
                        Listing
<HTML>
<HEAD>
 <TITLE>Listing 5.1</TITLE>
</HEAD>
<BODY BGCOLOR=WHITE>
 <APPLET CODEBASE="classes" CODE="Applet1.class"
 → WIDTH=400 HEIGHT=500>
 </APPLET>
</BODY>
</HTML>
```

Applet 5.1 Declaring, initializing, and using a string

```
                         Applet
/*
 Simple applet to show how to declare variables
*/

import java.awt.*;
import java.applet.Applet;

public class Applet1 extends Applet{
  String stringVarWithValue = "Hey, I'm a
  → string!";
  Font f = new Font("TimesRoman",Font.BOLD,36);

  public void init() {
    setBackground(Color.white);
  }

  public void paint(Graphics g) {
    g.setFont(f);
    g.drawString(this.stringVarWithValue, 50 ,
    → 150);
  }

}
```

Figure 5.1 There's our string, big as life!

Listing 5.2 This HTML file calls Applet 5.2.

```
                    Listing
<HTML>
<HEAD>
 <TITLE>Listing 5.2</TITLE>
</HEAD>
<BODY BGCOLOR=WHITE>
 <APPLET CODEBASE="classes" CODE="Applet2.class"
 → WIDTH=400 HEIGHT=500>
 </APPLET>
</BODY>
</HTML>
```

Applet 5.2 We add a little complexity by declaring the variable and setting it in two different places.

```
                    Applet
/*
 Ways of declaring and initializing strings
*/

import java.awt.*;
import java.applet.Applet;

public class Applet2 extends Applet{
 String stringVar;
 String stringVarWithValue = "Hey, I'm a
 → string!";
 Font f = new Font("TimesRoman",Font.BOLD,36);

 public void init() {
   setBackground(Color.white);
 }

 public void paint(Graphics g) {
   this.stringVar = "Now I have a value.";

   g.setFont(f);
   g.drawString(this.stringVar, 50 , 50);
   g.drawString(this.stringVarWithValue, 50 ,
   → 100);
 }

}
```

Figure 5.2 But when they're both displayed on the screen, both string variables appear the same.

More about strings

You don't always have to initialize (give a value to) a string when you declare it. Sometimes, you know that you'll need it later, but you don't yet know what value it will have. Here's an example of a string that's declared as part of the class, but not initialized until we use the paint() method.

To declare a string variable without initialization:

1. String stringVar;

   This line creates a new string variable, which we'll call stringVar.

2. this.stringVar = "Now I have a value.";

   Now, down in the paint() method, we've finally decided what value we want this string to have.

3. g.drawString(this.stringVar, 50 , 50);

   Now that stringVar has been both declared and initialized, there's no difference between it and our other string variable.

✔ Tip

■ If you declare a variable without setting it, it will be equal to null (nothing) until you do set it. Null is not the same as ""; that's an empty string, but it does have a value. Null means that no value has been set for this variable at all. To check to see if stringVar hasn't been set, your code should, if necessary, check if (stringVar == null).

Variable scope

No, this doesn't mean that we have variables that need to use mouthwash, although errors with variable scope have been known to make programmers get their mouths washed out with soap.

In this example, as shown in Listing 5.3 and Applet 5.3, a variable with the same name can be declared both at the class level and at the method level. You and your code can then become very confused as to which variable you mean.

To demonstrate scope:

1. String stringVar;

   This line declares the variable for the Applet3 class.

2. String stringVar = "I'm a local variable";

   This line, within the paint() method, creates and initializes an entirely new variable with no relation to the other, even though they have the same name.

3. g.drawString(stringVar, 50 , 50);

   This line displays the local variable, the variable which appears at the method level, which has a value, as shown in Figure 5.3.

4. g.drawString(this.stringVar, 50 , 100);

   Because of the "this." before the stringVar, this variable gets its value from outside of the method. Because this particular variable hasn't been set, nothing prints on this line.

Listing 5.3 This HTML file calls Applet 5.3.

```
<HTML>
<HEAD>
 <TITLE>Listing 5.3</TITLE>
</HEAD>
<BODY BGCOLOR=WHITE>
 <APPLET CODEBASE="classes" CODE="Applet3.class"
 → WIDTH=400 HEIGHT=500>
 </APPLET>
</BODY>
</HTML>
```

Applet 5.3 This applet demonstrates a type of problem that can cause you hours of frustration: variable scope.

```
/*
 This applet demonstrates scope
*/

import java.awt.*;
import java.applet.Applet;

public class Applet3 extends Applet{
 String stringVar;
 String stringVarWithValue = "Hey, I'm a
 → string!";
 Font f = new Font("TimesRoman",Font.BOLD,36);

 public void init() {
 setBackground(Color.white);
 }

 public void paint(Graphics g) {
   String stringVar = "I'm a local variable";

   g.setFont(f);
   g.drawString(stringVar, 50 , 50);
   g.drawString(this.stringVar, 50 , 100);
   g.drawString(this.stringVarWithValue, 50 ,
   → 150);
 }
}
```

Figure 5.3 Which stringVar variable has which value?

What is Scope?

In most of the world, when you talk about "Broadway," people know that you're referring to a street in New York City. While the street itself is in New York, people globally understand where you're referring to. You can think of Broadway as a global.

However, if you're in San Diego, California, and you refer to "Broadway," people will think that you're referring to a major street in their downtown area. This is a local value. In San Diego, not being clear about whether you're referring to the locally-known "Broadway" or the globally-known "Broadway" can lead to confusion.

If you're in San Diego, the default is the local version, and you have to explicitly state "New York City's Broadway" in order to refer to the other. Outside of San Diego, people will think of New York's Broadway first, unless they have some other local version of Broadway.

The "scope" of each of these streets is where each is the default, that is, the one that will be automatically thought of if no other identifying information is given. The scope of San Diego's Broadway is local—inside the city and a few outlying suburbs. The scope of New York's Broadway is global, that is, people anywhere in the world will know where you're referring to.

With software, the easiest way to avoid questions about a variable's scope is to avoid using two variables with the same name in two different places doing two different things. If you must go down this slippery slope, be clear about your variable's scope!

✔ Tips

- In this example, the "this." in the last g.drawstring() call isn't required. Java would still be able to find the correct variable to display without it. However, including it lets you keep better track of what you're doing, so examples in this book will always use this style.

- The best way to avoid problems with scope is to be very careful with giving two variables the same name. A simple mistake here can lead to hours of debugging headaches.

String Methods

A variety of string methods (that is, methods that apply to strings) are built into Java. Listing 5.4 and Applet 5.4 show what a few of them can do.

To use string methods:

1. g.drawString("The string is: \"
→ "+this.stringVar+"\"", 50 , 75);

If we want to display quotes in Java, they must be escaped. That is, if the code is just """, Java won't understand that we want to display the center one. Putting the backslash in front of a character tells Java to just pass it right on through, don't interpret it. We can't just say "The string is: " " and expect Java to know that the second quote is something we want to print, but the first and third are the beginning and end of a string. So, we *escape* the quote character—we tell Java to pretend that it doesn't see the next character—by putting a / (slash) before it.

2. g.drawString("The string's length is:
→ "+this.stringVar.length(), 50 , 100);

Once we have declared a string in Java, we automatically inherit some methods. One of these is length(), which we can use to get the length of a string; in this case, the result is 18, as shown in Figure 5.4.

3. g.drawString("Lower case:
→ "+this.stringVar.toLowerCase(), 50 , 125);

Another string method is toLowerCase(), which does just what it sounds like it does: causes every character in the string, whether upper- or lowercase, to be displayed in lowercase letters.

4. g.drawString("Upper case:
→ "+this.stringVar.toUpperCase(), 50 , 150);

And of course, if there's a toLowerCase(), there must be a toUpperCase(), which displays the string in all uppercase letters.

Listing 5.4. This HTML file calls Applet 5.4.

```
                        Listing
<HTML>
<HEAD>
 <TITLE>Listing 5.4</TITLE>
</HEAD>
<BODY BGCOLOR=WHITE>
 <APPLET CODEBASE="classes" CODE="Applet4.class"
 → WIDTH=400 HEIGHT=500>
 </APPLET>
</BODY>
</HTML>
```

Applet 5.4 This applet displays some of the most common string methods.

```
                        Applet
/*
 A demonstration of some string methods
*/

import java.awt.*;
import java.applet.Applet;

public class Applet4 extends Applet{
  String stringVar = "Hey, I'm a string!";
  Font f = new Font("TimesRoman",Font.BOLD,20);

  public void init() {
    setBackground(Color.white);
  }

  public void paint(Graphics g) {
    g.setFont(f);
    g.drawString("The string is: "+this.stringVar,
    →50 , 50);
    g.drawString("The string is: \""+this.string
    →Var+"\"", 50 , 75);
    g.drawString("The string's length is:
    → "+this.stringVar.length(), 50 , 100);
    g.drawString("Lower case: "+this.stringVar.
    →toLowerCase(), 50 , 125);
    g.drawString("Upper case: "+this.stringVar.
    →toUpperCase(), 50 , 150);
  }

}
```

Figure 5.4 Here's the string, its length, and how it looks in all lowercase and all uppercase.

✔ Tip

- Using these methods does not change the value of the string! For example, the toLowerCase() method simply displays the string in all lowercase letters; it does not change the value of the string itself.

All types of numbers

Java has six different types of numeric variables. (Those readers who are familiar with JavaScript will find this a little odd, as JavaScript only has one numeric variable type.) Listing 5.5 and Applet 5.5 show the maximum value of each type.

To declare numeric variables:

1. byte myByte = Byte.MAX_VALUE;
short myShort = Short.MAX_VALUE;
int myInt = Integer.MAX_VALUE;
long myLong = Long.MAX_VALUE;
float myFloat = Float.MAX_VALUE;
double myDouble = Double.MAX_VALUE;

In this step, we declare one of each of the six types of numeric variable, and simultaneously initialize it to the maximum value for its type.

2. g.drawString("The maximum value of a byte
→ is: "+this.myByte, 10 , 20);
g.drawString("The maximum value of a short
→ is: "+this.myShort, 10 , 40);
g.drawString("The maximum value of an
→ integer is: "+this.myInt, 10 , 60);
g.drawString("The maximum value of a long
→ is: "+this.myLong, 10 , 80);
g.drawString("The maximum value of a float
→ is: "+this.myFloat, 10 , 100);
g.drawString("The maximum value of a
→ double is: "+this.myDouble, 10 , 120);

The above lines display the maximum value for each of the numeric variable types, as shown in Figure 5.5. Which you use depends on what range of values you think that variable will need to hold.

The range of values for each numeric type is shown in Table 5.1. For the most part, you'll be using integers, with the occasional switch to float (also known as floating point) variables when decimal values are required.

Listing 5.5 This HTML file calls Applet 5.5.

```
Listing
<HTML>
<HEAD>
 <TITLE>Listing 5.5</TITLE>
</HEAD>
<BODY BGCOLOR=WHITE>
 <APPLET CODEBASE="classes" CODE="Applet5.class"
 → WIDTH=500 HEIGHT=500>
 </APPLET>
</BODY>
</HTML>
```

Applet 5.5 This applet declares and initializes an example of each of the six numeric types, and also displays their largest values.

```
Applet
/*
 This applet demonstrates the different types of
 numbers in Java
*/

import java.awt.*;
import java.applet.Applet;

public class Applet5 extends Applet{
 byte myByte = Byte.MAX_VALUE;
 short myShort = Short.MAX_VALUE;
 int myInt = Integer.MAX_VALUE;
 long myLong = Long.MAX_VALUE;
 float myFloat = Float.MAX_VALUE;
 double myDouble = Double.MAX_VALUE;

 Font f = new Font("TimesRoman",Font.BOLD,16);

 public void init() {
   setBackground(Color.white);
 }

 public void paint(Graphics g) {
   g.setFont(f);
   g.drawString("The maximum value of a byte is:
   → "+this.myByte, 10 , 20);
   g.drawString("The maximum value of a short is:
   → "+this.myShort, 10 , 40);
   g.drawString("The maximum value of an integer
   → is: "+this.myInt, 10 , 60);
   g.drawString("The maximum value of a long is:
   → "+this.myLong, 10 , 80);
   g.drawString("The maximum value of a float is:
   → "+this.myFloat, 10 , 100);
   g.drawString("The maximum value of a double
   → is: "+this.myDouble, 10 , 120);
 }

}
```

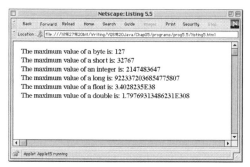

Figure 5.5 Bytes are small, doubles are huge, and here's everything in between.

Table 5.1

Range of Numeric Types	
TYPE	**RANGE**
Byte	-128 to 127
Short	-32768 to 32767
Integer	-2147483648 to 2147483647
Long	-9223372036854775808 to 9223372036854775807
Float	-1.40239846E-45 to 3.4028235E38
Double	4.94065645841246544E-324 to 1.79769313486231E308

✔ Tips

- No, your eyes aren't deceiving you. There is a difference between byte and Byte, between short and Short, and so on. The first of each pair (in all lowercase) is what Java refers to as a "primitive." This means that, while it can be passed in and out of methods and assigned to variables, it is not actually an object with methods of its own. In order to use the MAX_VALUE constant for each numeric object, we have to refer instead to its associated primitive class.

- For a number to be displayed using g.drawString(), the number must be converted to a string. Handily enough, concatenating a number to a string (via the "+" operator) is enough to do the job.

Converting between strings and numbers

Often, you'll need to convert a number to a string (to display it using a string method, for instance), or a string to a number (to apply a math calculation, perhaps). Java makes this simple and straightforward, as shown in Listing 5.6 and Applet 5.6.

To convert between strings and numbers:

1. this.myString = this.myInt.toString();

Converting a number to a string is as simple as calling the **toString()** method. This does not change the number itself to a string, it just returns the numeric value in string form.

2. g.drawString("And converted back like this: "
→ +Integer.valueOf(this.my String), 10, 100);

The String class doesn't contain a method to turn itself into numbers, so we have to use the Integer method **valueOf()**. This returns the integer value of the string if it contains a valid number, or an error otherwise. Once converted the now-numeric String is displayed, as shown in Figure 5.6.

✔ Tip

■ Note the difference between the previous task and this example in the way we declare myInt. In the previous example, we were declaring myInt to be an instance of the primitive type **int**, and in this case, myInt is an instance of the class **Integer**. The value of the variable is the same, but making it an instance of the Integer class allows us to use that class's methods.

Listing 5.6. This HTML file calls Applet 5.6.

```
<HTML>
<HEAD>
 <TITLE>Listing 5.6</TITLE>
</HEAD>
<BODY BGCOLOR=WHITE>
 <APPLET CODEBASE="classes" CODE="Applet6.class"
 → WIDTH=500 HEIGHT=500>
 </APPLET>
</BODY>
</HTML>
```

Applet 5.6 Here's how we go from numbers to strings and back again.

```
/*
  This applet demonstrates how to convert numbers
  to strings and back again
*/

import java.awt.*;
import java.applet.Applet;

public class Applet6 extends Applet{
  Integer myInt = new Integer(Integer.MAX_VALUE);
  → String myString;
  Font f = new Font("TimesRoman",Font.BOLD,16);

  public void init() {
    setBackground(Color.white);
  }

  public void paint(Graphics g) {
    g.setFont(f);
    g.drawString("The maximum value of an integer
    → is: "+this.myInt, 10 , 40);
    g.drawString("And it can be displayed as a
    →string like this: ", 10, 60);
    this.myString = this.myInt.toString();
    g.drawString(this.myString, 10, 80);
    g.drawString("And converted back like this:
    → "+Integer.valueOf(this.myString), 10, 100);
  }

}
```

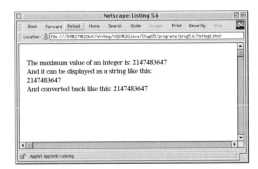

Figure 5.6 The biggest integer value, converted to a string and then back to an integer.

Listing 5.7 This HTML file calls Applet 5.7.

```
Listing
<HTML>
<HEAD>
  <TITLE>Listing 5.7</TITLE>
</HEAD>
<BODY BGCOLOR=WHITE>
  <APPLET CODEBASE="classes" CODE="Applet7.class"
  → WIDTH=500 HEIGHT=500>
  </APPLET>
</BODY>
</HTML>
```

Applet 5.7 Java provides straightforward ways of converting between types of numbers.

```
Applet
/*
  This applet demonstrates type conversion via
  object methods
*/

import java.awt.*;
import java.applet.Applet;

public class Applet7 extends Applet{
  Double myDouble = new Double(Math.PI);
  Byte myByte = new Byte(myDouble.byteValue());
  Short myShort = new Short(myDouble.shortValue
  → ());
  Integer myInt = new Integer(myDouble.intValue
  → ());
  Long myLong = new Long(myDouble.longValue());
  Float myFloat =
  → new Float(myDouble.floatValue());

  Font f = new Font("TimesRoman",Font.BOLD,16);

  public void init() {
    setBackground(Color.white);
  }

  public void paint(Graphics g) {
    g.setFont(f);
    g.drawString("The value of pi as a byte is: "
    →+this.myByte, 10 , 20);
    g.drawString("The value of pi as a short is: "
    →+this.myShort, 10 , 40);
    g.drawString("The value of pi as an integer
    → is: "+this.myInt, 10 , 60);
    g.drawString("The value of pi as a long is: "
    →+this.myLong, 10 , 80);
    g.drawString("The value of pi as a float is: "
    →+this.myFloat, 10 , 100);
    g.drawString("The value of pi as a double is: "
    →+this.myDouble, 10 , 120);
  }

}
```

Figure 5.7 All of our pieces of pi.

Converting between types of numbers

Given that Java has six different ways of storing numbers, you'll occasionally need to convert numbers from one form to another. Listing 5.7 and Applet 5.7 show you how to do this using the methods inherited from the Double object.

To convert numbers from one type to another:

1. Double myDouble = new Double(Math.PI);

This line declares a new object, myDouble, of type Double, and initializes it to the value of pi.

2. Byte myByte = new Byte(myDouble.
  → byteValue());
Short myShort = newShort(myDouble.
  → shortValue());
Integer myInt = new Integer(myDouble.
  → intValue());
Long myLong = new Long(myDouble.
  → longValue());
Float myFloat = new Float(myDouble.
  → floatValue());

These five lines declare five numeric objects, one of each of the sixtypes (when you include Double). Each is initialized to the value of myDouble, modified by the appropriate method for its type.

✔ Tips

■ Converting a number from float or double to any of the other types simply truncates the decimal portion of the number, as shown in Figure 5.7.

Converting by casting

Another technique for converting between variable types is called "casting." This style of conversion enables you to get the value in a different format without actually creating a new object or converting the old object. Applet 5.8 demonstrates casting.

To cast one type to another:

1. g.drawString("The value of pi as a byte is: "
   → +(byte)this.myDouble, 10 , 20);
   g.drawString("The value of pi as a short is: "
   → +(short)this.myDouble, 10 , 40);
   g.drawString("The value of pi as an integer
   → is: "+(int)this.myDouble, 10 , → 60);
   g.drawString("The value of pi as a long is: "
   → +(long)this.myDouble, 10 , 80);
   g.drawString("The value of pi as a float is: "
   → +(float)this.myDouble, 10 , 100);

   This applet starts off much like the previous example (Applet 5.7) but only declares and initializes the double object myDouble.

   When it comes time to print the value of each, this.myDouble is printed each time, but cast to the type that we're looking for. To cast a variable as another type, you put the type desired within parentheses just before the value that you have. For instance, (short)this.myDouble returns a short.

✔ Tip

- Java allows you to cast objects into other objects, but requires that they be related by inheritance—one must be either a subclass or a superclass of the other.

- Note that in this example myDouble is declared as the primitive double, not the object Double. Also, the type that we're casting each object into is the primitive version, not the object version, of the type. This is required because Java will not allow you to cast primitive types to objects, or vice versa.

Listing 5.8 This HTML file calls Applet 5.8.

```
                    Listing
<HTML>
<HEAD>
 <TITLE>Listing 5.8</TITLE>
</HEAD>
<BODY BGCOLOR=WHITE>
 <APPLET CODEBASE="classes" CODE="Applet8.class"
 → WIDTH=500 HEIGHT=500>
 </APPLET>
</BODY>
</HTML>
```

Applet 5.8 Using casting to convert a number from one type to another

```
                    Applet
/*
 Simple applet to demonstrate casting
*/

import java.awt.*;
import java.applet.Applet;

public class Applet8 extends Applet{
  double myDouble = Math.PI;
  Font f = new Font("TimesRoman",Font.BOLD,16);

  public void init() {
    setBackground(Color.white);
  }

  public void paint(Graphics g) {
    g.setFont(f);
    g.drawString("The value of pi as a byte is: "
    →+(byte)this.myDouble, 10 , 20);
    g.drawString("The value of pi as a short is: "
    →+(short)this.myDouble, 10 , 40);
    g.drawString("The value of pi as an integer
    → is: "+(int)this.myDouble, 10 , 60);
    g.drawString("The value of pi as a long is: "
    →+(long)this.myDouble, 10 , 80);
    g.drawString("The value of pi as a float is: "
    →+(float)this.myDouble, 10 , 100);
    g.drawString("The value of pi as a double is: "
    →+this.myDouble, 10 , 120);
  }

}
```

Figure 5.8 More pieces of pi

CONVERTING BY CASTING

Listing 5.9 This HTML file calls Applet 5.9.

```
<HTML>
<HEAD>
 <TITLE>Listing 5.9</TITLE>
</HEAD>
<BODY BGCOLOR=WHITE>
 <APPLET CODEBASE="classes" CODE="Applet9.class"
 → WIDTH=500 HEIGHT=500>
 </APPLET>
</BODY>
</HTML>
```

Applet 5.9 Using arrays to avoid having to create
multiple identical objects

```
/*
 Simple applet to demonstrate arrays
*/

import java.awt.*;
import java.applet.Applet;

public class Applet9 extends Applet{
 String[] dayOfTheWeek = {"Sunday","Monday",
 →"Tuesday","Wednesday","Thursday","Friday",
 →"Saturday"};
 String[] ordinalNumber = {"first","second",
 →"third","fourth","fifth","sixth","seventh"};
 Font f = new Font("TimesRoman",Font.BOLD,16);

 public void init() {
 setBackground(Color.white);
 }

 public void paint(Graphics g) {
  g.setFont(f);

  g.drawString("The "+ordinalNumber[0]+" day of
  → the week is "+dayOfTheWeek[0], 10 , 20);
  g.drawString("The "+ordinalNumber[1]+" day of
  → the week is "+dayOfTheWeek[1], 10 , 40);
  g.drawString("The "+ordinalNumber[2]+" day of
  → the week is "+dayOfTheWeek[2], 10 , 60);
  g.drawString("The "+ordinalNumber[3]+" day of
  → the week is "+dayOfTheWeek[3], 10 , 80);
  g.drawString("The "+ordinalNumber[4]+" day of
  → the week is "+dayOfTheWeek[4], 10 ,100);
  g.drawString("The "+ordinalNumber[5]+" day of
  → the week is "+dayOfTheWeek[5], 10 ,120);
  g.drawString("The "+ordinalNumber[6]+" day of
  → the week is "+dayOfTheWeek[6], 10 ,140);
 }

}
```

Arrays of objects

Often, you'll want to use several related
objects of the same type. Instead of declaring
different variables for each, you can declare
one variable as an array, which then contains
multiple values. In Listing 5.9 and Applet 5.9,
we use arrays to display the days of the week.

To use arrays:

1. String[] dayOfTheWeek = {"Sunday",
   → "Monday", "Tuesday", "Wednesday",
   → "Thursday", "Friday", "Saturday"};

   This line declares and initializes an array of
   type String, with the name dayOfTheWeek.
   The square brackets after "String" signify
   that what follows is an array. Each of the
   values within the curly brackets is assigned
   to the array. In this case, there are seven
   elements in the array, which are referred
   to as elements 0 through 6.

2. String[] ordinalNumber = {"first", "second",
   → "third", "fourth", "fifth", "sixth",
   → "seventh"};

   Here we declare and initialize another
   string array, this one named ordinalNumber.

3. g.drawString("The " + ordinalNumber[0]+" day
   of the week is "+dayOfTheWeek[0], 10 , 20);

   This line prints out that the "first" day of
   the week is "Sunday". Remember, the first
   element of the array is at position 0.

4. g.drawString("The " + ordinalNumber [1]+"
   → day of the week is "+dayOfTheWeek[1],
   → 10, 40);
   g.drawString("The " + ordinalNumber [2]+"
   → day of the week is "+dayOfTheWeek[2],
   → 10, 60);
   g.drawString("The " + ordinalNumber [3]+"
   → day of the week is "+dayOfTheWeek[3],
   → 10, 80);
   g.drawString("The " + ordinalNumber[4]+"
   → day of the week is "+dayOfTheWeek[4],
   → 10, 100);

```
g.drawString("The " + ordinalNumber[5]+"
→ day of the week is "+dayOfTheWeek[5],
→ 10,120);
g.drawString("The " + ordinalNumber[6]+"
→ day of the week is "+dayOfTheWeek[6],
→ 10,140);
```

These lines print out the rest of the days of the week (array elements 1 through 6), as shown in Figure 5.9.

✔ Tips

- Looking at this example, you might think that because all of the g.drawString() lines are virtually identical, there ought to be a way to write this code with less repetition. You'll learn how in Chapter 6, where you'll revisit this example as you learn about loops.

- Each element of an array is still a variable of its own, and can be modified independently of the others.

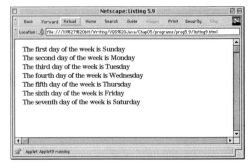

Figure 5.9 Here are the days of the week.

DECISIONS, DECISIONS

Java applets don't always flow straight through from beginning to end. Sometimes, it's necessary to skip a segment of code, or to execute the same segment more than once. This is called *flow control*—controlling the way the applet flows through your code. In this chapter, you'll see how to make your code follow your directions.

Conditionals: the if statement

The simplest way to control the code that is executed in your applet is with the if statement. This command simply says, "if some value is true, then execute the commands within the following braces. Otherwise, skip this code." Listing 6.1 and Applet 6.1 show you how to use conditionals to program a simple "guess a number" game.

To use an "if" statement:

1. public class Applet1 extends Applet {

   Our new applet is called **Applet1**, and is defined as extending the **Applet** class.

2. TextField guessField = new TextField(5);
   int nextGuess = -1;

   The variable **guessField** is defined as type **TextField**, with a length of 5. This is the text entry box where the user will enter their guesses. The variable **nextGuess** is where we'll be storing the values that the user enters, so we'll start it off as -1. That number isn't a valid guess, so we'll use it as a flag to show we're just starting out.

3. int targetNum =
   → (int)(java.lang.Math.random() * 100)+1;
   Font f = new Font
   → ("TimesRoman",Font.BOLD,24);

   The Java method java.lang.Math.random() generates a random number between 0 and 1 (for example, .722 or .111). We then multiply this number by 100 (resulting in 72.2 or 11.1). Finally, we take its integer value (that is, we strip off everything from the decimal point rightwards) to produce a result between 0 and 99. We then add 1 to the number to get a result between 1 and 100, and store it in the variable **targetNum**. Both **nextGuess** and **targetNum** are of type int.

Listing 6.1 This HTML calls the applet inside the browser window.

```
Listing
<HTML>
<HEAD>
 <TITLE>Listing 6.1</TITLE>
</HEAD>
<BODY BGCOLOR=WHITE>
 <APPLET CODEBASE="classes" CODE="Applet1.class"
 → WIDTH=500 HEIGHT=100>
 </APPLET>
</BODY>
</HTML>
```

Applet 6.1 Let's play a game of "guess the number."

```
Applet
import java.awt.*;
import java.applet.Applet;
import java.awt.Font;

public class Applet1 extends Applet {
  TextField guessField = new TextField(5);
  int nextGuess = -1;
  int targetNum = (int)(java.lang.Math.random
  → () * 100)+1;
  Font f = new Font("TimesRoman",Font.BOLD,24);

  public void init() {
    setBackground(Color.white);
    add(guessField);
  }

  public void paint(Graphics g) {
    String numberStatus = nextGuess + " is
    → correct";

    g.setFont(f);
    if (nextGuess != targetNum) {
      numberStatus = nextGuess + " is not
      → correct";
    }
    if (nextGuess < 1) {
      numberStatus = "Guess a number between 1
      → and 100";
    }
    g.drawString(numberStatus, 20, 60);
  }

  public boolean action(Event e, Object arg) {
    if (e.target instanceof TextField) {
      try {
        nextGuess = Integer.parseInt
        → (guessField.getText());
      }
      catch (NumberFormatException x) {
        nextGuess = -1;
      }
      repaint();
      return true;
    }
    return false;
  }
}
```

Figure 6.1 Here the applet tells the user what they're expected to do.

Figure 6.2 "Sorry, that number wasn't correct."

Figure 6.3 Finally, the user guessed the correct number!

Lastly, we create a new font variable f, which is set to 24-point bold Times Roman.

4.
```
public void init() {
    setBackground(Color.white);
    add(guessField);
}
```

This is a simple init() method (as described in Chapter 4) that sets the background of the applet to white and puts the guessField text box in the window.

5.
```
public void paint(Graphics g) {
    String numberStatus = nextGuess + " is
    → correct";
    g.setFont(f);
```

We start off the paint() method by defining a new String, numberStatus. It's initialized to a value of nextGuess followed by a message that assumes that nextGuess was correct, as shown in Figure 6.3. Then we set the window's font to f.

6.
```
if (nextGuess != targetNum) {
    numberStatus = nextGuess + " is not
    → correct";
}
```

Here's our first if statement. This code checks to see if nextGuess is not equal to targetNum, i.e., if the number the user entered doesn't match the number that we're looking for. If this is true—that is, if the numbers don't match—then we execute the code within the curly braces. Otherwise, we do nothing. In this case, if the two are different, numberStatus is reset to say that the user entered a number that was not correct, as seen in Figure 6.2.

7.
```
if (nextGuess < 1) {
    numberStatus = "Guess a number between
    → 1 and 100";
}
```

CONDITIONALS: THE IF STATEMENT

Here's another if statement. In this one, we check to see if nextGuess is less than 1, which is our flag that an invalid value was entered. In this case, we remind the user what it is we're expecting to see. Figure 6.1 shows this in action.

8. g.drawString(numberStatus, 20, 60);
}

This code displays whatever value numberStatus was set to (reflecting whether the user-entered value was correct, incorrect, or invalid). The curly brace ends the paint() method.

9. public boolean action(Event e, Object arg) {
    if (e.target instanceof TextField) {

Here's where some action finally occurs: in the action() method. This method is invoked when the user enters something into the text field. The action() method returns true or false, depending on whether or not we're completely handling the processing in this method. First, we check to see if the event that caused the action() method to run is one that the method knows how to handle. The only event we're going to handle here is a change to the text field, so we check if the target of the event is an instance of TextField. If so, we handle the event, otherwise we'll later return false.

10. try {
        nextGuess = Integer.parseInt(guessField.
        ⇥ getText());
    }
    catch (NumberFormatException x) {
        nextGuess = -1;
    }
    repaint();
    return true;

A try is a special kind of if statement. In this situation, we're going to attempt to execute a statement where there's a chance an error might occur. So we just

Java throws a tantrum

Think about a little kid throwing a tantrum: "I'm not going to eat my spinach, I'm not, I'm not, and you can't make me."

Java doesn't throw tantrums, but it can throw exceptions, which can be very similar. In both cases, you have a "do this or else!" situation, caused by an unexpected or unwanted event. The kid doesn't want to eat spinach, and in this example, Java doesn't want to turn letters into numbers.

With a small child, the "or else" depends on the kid. When Java throws an exception, you, the programmer, need to catch it (unlike that kid, who's going to catch it if he doesn't eat his veggies). The catch keyword tells Java what to do when possible exceptions have been thrown.

try the statement. If it's valid, everything's fine. If it's invalid, we throw an exception. Well, if an exception is thrown, it needs to be caught, which takes place in the catch statement. In this case, we're going to take what the user entered and turn it into a number. As the user could have entered anything, we put the attempt to convert the entered value to a number in a try statement. If the input can be turned into an integer, nextGuess is set to that number. If not, a NumberFormatException exception is thrown and then caught, which causes nextGuess to be set to -1. Either way, we call the repaint() method to redraw the window and return true to signify that the event was completely handled.

Otherwise, we return false to tell Java that it should handle any other events as it normally does.

✔ Tips

- If you've ever programmed in another language, you might be expecting to see a "then" after the "if." In Java, the "then" is just assumed to be there.

- It's common in Java to see an if statement followed by a single indented line with no curly braces. This is valid Java syntax, and means that the one line following the if is the sole statement to be executed when the if check is true. However, this book will use curly braces for clarity's sake.

- Yes, this is a very convoluted way to write this applet. On the average, a user would have to guess 50 or more numbers before they would pick the right one. The next example will show a better approach.

More conditionals: if/else statements

It makes sense that if you sometimes want code to be executed only if some value is true, and other times you'll want code to be executed only if a value is false. In this case, you use an else, which allows you to define a block of code that's executed only when the check in the if statement fails. Listing 6.2 and Applet 6.2 show an improved "guess a number" game where the user is given some feedback about how close their guess is to the correct answer.

To use an if/else construct:

1. if (nextGuess != targetNum) {

We start off by checking to see if the user's guess matches what the computer is expecting. The following block of code is only executed if the guess was incorrect.

2. if (nextGuess < 1) {
    numberStatus = "Guess a number between
    → 1 and 100";
}

First, we check to see if nextGuess has a value of -1, which occurs on the first pass through this code and when an invalid value was entered. If so, the message "Guess a number between 1 and 100" is displayed.

3.   else {

Otherwise, if nextGuess is not equal to targetNum, and nextGuess is a valid number, then we want to execute the statements in the else clause. In this case, the else clause consists of another if/else construct.

Listing 6.2. This calls Applet 6.2 inside the browser window.

```
Listing
<HTML>
<HEAD>
  <TITLE>Listing 6.2</TITLE>
</HEAD>
<BODY BGCOLOR=WHITE>
  <APPLET CODEBASE="classes" CODE="Applet2.class"
  → WIDTH=500 HEIGHT=100>
  </APPLET>
</BODY>
</HTML>
```

Applet 6.2 A better game of "guess the number"

```
Applet
import java.awt.*;
import java.applet.Applet;
import java.awt.Font;

public class Applet2 extends Applet {
  TextField guessField = new TextField(5);
  int nextGuess = -1;
  int targetNum = (int)(java.lang.Math.random() *
  →100)+1;
  Font f = new Font("TimesRoman",Font.BOLD,24);

  public void init() {
    setBackground(Color.white);
    add(guessField);
  }

  public void paint(Graphics g) {
    String numberStatus = nextGuess + " is
    → correct";

    g.setFont(f);
    if (nextGuess != targetNum) {
      if (nextGuess < 1) {
        numberStatus = "Guess a number between 1
        → and 100";
      }
      else {
        if (nextGuess < targetNum) {
          numberStatus = nextGuess + " is too low";
        }
        else {
          numberStatus = nextGuess + " is too
          → high";
        }
      }
    }
    g.drawString(numberStatus, 20, 60);
  }

  public boolean action(Event e, Object arg) {
    if (e.target instanceof TextField) {
      try {
        nextGuess =
        →Integer.parseInt(guessField.getText());
      }
      catch (NumberFormatException x) {
        nextGuess = -1;
      }
      repaint();
      return true;
    }
    return false;
  }
}
```

Figure 6.4 We'll start by guessing 50, and see whether we're high or low. In this case, 50 was too high.

Figure 6.5 Split the difference between 1 and 50, and try 25—in this case, too low.

Figure 6.6 Split the difference between 25 and 50, and try 37—still too low.

Figure 6.7 We split the difference between 37 and 50, but 43 is still too low.

Figure 6.8 Splitting the difference between 43 and 50, we find out that 46 is too high.

Figure 6.9 And the correct answer was 44!

4.
```
if (nextGuess < targetNum) {
    numberStatus = nextGuess + " is too
    → low";
}
else {
    numberStatus = nextGuess + " is too
    → high";
}
```

Here, we check if nextGuess is less than targetNum. If so, nextGuess is displayed, along with the message that it was too low, as in Figures 6.5, 6.6, and 6.7. Otherwise, the message displayed says that the entry was too high, as in Figures 6.4 and 6.8. If the entry matched targetNum, the message in Figure 6.9 is shown.

✔ Tip

- In the previous example, the user would have had to make 50 guesses to have a 50% chance of getting the right answer. In this example, the user should always be able to get the right answer within seven guesses.

Around and around with loops

With an if/else structure, you have code that you execute either once or not at all. Sometimes, though, you'll have code that you want to execute over and over again. This is called a "loop." Listing 6.3 and Applet 6.3 demonstrate one type of loop: the for loop. Here, we're going to let the user enter a number, and then print that many asterisks in the window.

To use a for loop:

1. if (userNum < 1 || userNum > 50) {
       outStr = "Enter a number between 1 and
   → 50";
   }

   First, we make sure that the user entered a valid number: It must be between 1 and 50.

2. else {
       for (i=0; i<userNum; i++) {
           outStr = outStr + "*";
       }
   }

   Otherwise, we execute the for loop. The first part of the for loop initializes the loop counter, i, to 0. The second part says to continue looping so long as i is less than the value the user entered. The third part says to add one to i every time the loop goes around. Figure 6.10 shows the result after the user has entered "29." The variable outStr starts empty and adds an asterisk to itself with each pass through the loop.

Listing 6.3 Calls Applet 6.3

```
Listing
<HTML>
<HEAD>
 <TITLE>Listing 6.3</TITLE>
</HEAD>
<BODY BGCOLOR=WHITE>
 <APPLET CODEBASE="classes" CODE="Applet3.class"
 → WIDTH=500 HEIGHT=100>
 </APPLET>
</BODY>
</HTML>
```

Applet 6.3 This applet asks the user for a number and then loops through that many times.

```
Applet
import java.awt.*;
import java.applet.Applet;
import java.awt.Font;

public class Applet3 extends Applet {
  TextField userField = new TextField(5);
  int userNum = -1;
  Font f = new Font("TimesRoman",Font.BOLD,24);

  public void init() {
    setBackground(Color.white);
    add(userField);
  }

  public void paint(Graphics g) {
    String outStr = "";
    int i;

    g.setFont(f);
    if (userNum < 1 || userNum > 50) {
      outStr = "Enter a number between 1 and 50";
    }
    else {
      for (i=0; i<userNum; i++) {
        outStr = outStr + "*";
      }
    }
    g.drawString(outStr, 20, 60);
  }

  public boolean action(Event e, Object arg) {
    if (e.target instanceof TextField) {
      try {
        userNum = Integer.parseInt(userField.
          ·getText());
      }
      catch (NumberFormatException x) {
        userNum = -1;
      }
      repaint();
      return true;
    }
    return false;
  }
}
```

Figure 6.10 The user asked for 29 asterisks, and that's what they got.

$$\underset{\text{Initialization}}{\underline{\texttt{i=0;}}} \quad \underset{\text{Limiting}}{\underline{\texttt{i<userNum;}}} \quad \underset{\text{Increment}}{\underline{\texttt{i++}}}$$

Figure 6.11 The three parts of a loop.

Looping the Loop

A for loop has three parts, as shown in Figure 6.11:

1. The initialization step. This is where the loop counter is defined. The first time through the loop, this is what the loop variable is set to.

2. The limiting step. This is where we say when to stop looping. While normal people count from one to ten, it's common in programming languages to count from zero to nine. In both cases, the code inside the loop is run ten times, but the latter method works better with languages (like Java) where arrays start with a zero-th position. That's why you'll see loops have a limitation of "less than userNum" instead of "less than or equal to userNum."

3. The increment step. This is where we say how much to increase the loop counter by one each pass through the loop. In this case, we add one each time through by using "++" to add one to i's value each time through the loop.

✔ Tip

■ The "||" characters between the check for userNum less than 1, and userNum greater than 50 are read as "or," which means that the following lines are executed if either part is true. If we wanted it to only happen if both were true, we'd use an "and" instead, which uses the "&&" syntax instead of the "||".

Another loop through loops: the while loop

Java has three different ways of doing loops. The first is the for loop, and the other two are variations on the while loop. With a while loop, as shown in Listing 6.4 and Applet 6.4, the loop continues to execute so long as the condition you're checking for is true. Once it's no longer true, the loop terminates. If, the first time you check the condition, the result is false, the loop is never executed at all.

To use a while loop:

1.
```
while (i < userNum) {
    outStr = outStr + "*";
    i++;
}
```

The variable userNum is either a number between 1 and 50 (all valid values), or it's -1 (when an invalid entry was made). As i is initialized to be 0, this loop will never be executed when userNum is invalid, as 0 is never less than -1. If userNum is valid, the loop will be executed that many times, as shown in Figure 6.12. Each time through the loop, i is incremented by one. For instance, if userNum is 25, this loop will be run 25 times. If userNum is -1, the while loop will initially check if 0 is less than -1. As it isn't, the loop will never be entered.

✔ Tip

■ Make sure that you have some way of ending a while loop! For instance, if you left off the "i++;" in the above example, you'd create what's called an "infinite loop": one that has no way of ending itself (at least not until it crashes your machine).

Listing 6.4. Set up Applet 6.4 to be executed.

```
Listing
<HTML>
<HEAD>
 <TITLE>Listing 6.4</TITLE>
</HEAD>
<BODY BGCOLOR=WHITE>
 <APPLET CODEBASE="classes" CODE="Applet4.class"
 → WIDTH=500 HEIGHT=100>
 </APPLET>
</BODY>
</HTML>
```

Applet 6.4. How many asterisks does the user want to display?

```
Applet
import java.awt.*;
import java.applet.Applet;
import java.awt.Font;

public class Applet4 extends Applet {
  TextField userField = new TextField(5);
  int userNum = -1;
  Font f = new Font("TimesRoman",Font.BOLD,24);

  public void init() {
    setBackground(Color.white);
    add(userField);
  }

  public void paint(Graphics g) {
    String outStr = "";
    int i = 0;

    g.setFont(f);
    if (userNum > 50) {
      userNum = -1;
    }
    if (userNum < 1) {
      outStr = "Enter a number between 1 and 50";
    }
    while (i < userNum) {
      outStr = outStr + "*";
      i++;
    }
    g.drawString(outStr, 20, 60);
  }

  public boolean action(Event e, Object arg) {
    if (e.target instanceof TextField) {
      try {
        userNum = Integer.parseInt(userField.
        →getText());
      }
      catch (NumberFormatException x) {
        userNum = -1;
      }
      repaint();
      return true;
    }
    return false;
  }
}
```

Figure 6.12. In this case, the user only wanted three.

Listing 6.5 Calls Applet 6.5

```
                  Listing
<HTML>
<HEAD>
 <TITLE>Listing 6.5</TITLE>
</HEAD>
<BODY BGCOLOR=WHITE>
 <APPLET CODEBASE="classes" CODE="Applet5.class"
 → WIDTH=500 HEIGHT=100>
 </APPLET>
</BODY>
</HTML>
```

Applet 6.5 Using a do/while loop to process the user's request

```
                  Applet
import java.awt.*;
import java.applet.Applet;
import java.awt.Font;

public class Applet5 extends Applet {
 TextField userField = new TextField(5);
 int userNum = -1;
 Font f = new Font("TimesRoman",Font.BOLD,24);

 public void init() {
   setBackground(Color.white);
   add(userField);
 }

 public void paint(Graphics g) {
   String outStr = "";
   int i = 0;

   g.setFont(f);
   if (userNum < 1 || userNum > 50) {
     outStr = "Enter a number between 1 and 50";
   }
   else {
     do {
       outStr = outStr + "*";
       i++;
     } while (i < userNum);
   }
   g.drawString(outStr, 20, 60);
 }

 public boolean action(Event e, Object arg) {
   if (e.target instanceof TextField) {
     try {
       userNum =
       →Integer.parseInt(userField.getText());
     }
     catch (NumberFormatException x) {
       userNum = -1;
     }
     repaint();
     return true;
   }
   return false;
 }
}
```

Figure 6.13 The user requested 34 asterisks.

The last loop: the do/while loop

The last kind of Java loop is the do/while loop. In this format, the check for continuing the loop is at the end of the loop, instead of at the beginning. This means that the loop will always execute at least once. Listing 6.5 and Applet 6.5 demonstrate the do/while loop.

To use a do/while loop:

1. do {
　　outStr = outStr + "*";
　　i++;
　} while (i < userNum);

With this construct, outStr will always have at least one asterisk, so we want to be careful about how we get to this area of the code. In other words, you'll want to check if userNum is -1 before you start this loop. So long as i is less than userNum, this loop will continue to execute, as shown in Figure 6.13.

Take a break from loops

It's possible to be inside a loop, but encounter a condition under which you want to leave the loop immediately. This is called a "break."

In Listing 6.6 and Applet 6.6, the user is allowed to enter any number they like. However, no matter how large the number, the loop is limited to 20 times around.

To break from a loop:

1. for (i=0; i<userNum; i++) {
    if (i >= 20) break;
    outStr = outStr + "*";
}

This is a standard for loop, which would normally loop around until i was equal to userNum. The addition of the break in the middle, however, causes the loop to always exit when i reaches 20.

The break command causes execution to jump to the first line after the loop, as shown in Figure 6.14.

✔ Tip

■ Java also has a continue command. When you use continue, the remaining lines in the loop are skipped and execution resumes at the start of the loop.

Listing 6.6. Sets up Applet 6.6

```
<HTML>
<HEAD>
 <TITLE>Listing 6.6</TITLE>
</HEAD>
<BODY BGCOLOR=WHITE>
 <APPLET CODEBASE="classes" CODE="Applet6.class"
  → WIDTH=500 HEIGHT=100>
 </APPLET>
</BODY>
</HTML>
```

Applet 6.6 Demonstrates the use of a break to exit a loop

```
import java.awt.*;
import java.applet.Applet;
import java.awt.Font;

public class Applet6 extends Applet {
 TextField userField = new TextField(5);
 int userNum = -1;
 Font f = new Font("TimesRoman",Font.BOLD,24);

 public void init() {
   setBackground(Color.white);
   add(userField);
 }

 public void paint(Graphics g) {
   String outStr = "";
   int i;

   g.setFont(f);
   if (userNum < 1) {
     outStr = "Enter a number between 1 and 20";
   }
   else {
     for (i=0; i<userNum; i++) {
       if (i >= 20) break;
       outStr = outStr + "*";
     }
   }
   g.drawString(outStr, 20, 60);
 }

 public boolean action(Event e, Object arg) {
   if (e.target instanceof TextField) {
     try {
       userNum = Integer.parseInt(userField.
        →getText());
     }
     catch (NumberFormatException x) {
       userNum = -1;
     }
     repaint();
     return true;
   }
   return false;
 }
}
```

Figure 6.14 No matter what number we put in, the maximum is really 20.

Listing 6.7 Sets up the game in Applet 6.7

```
<HTML>
<HEAD>
 <TITLE>Listing 6.7</TITLE>
</HEAD>
<BODY BGCOLOR=WHITE>
 <APPLET CODEBASE="classes" CODE="Applet7.class"
 → WIDTH=500 HEIGHT=100>
 </APPLET>
</BODY>
</HTML>
```

The case with case

Java provides one more way for you to control the flow of your code: the switch/case statement. The easiest way to understand the switch/case statement is to think of it as a shorthand way of combining a whole bunch of if/else statements. Instead of saying "if today is Monday do this, else if today is Tuesday do some other thing, else if today is Wednesday do something else entirely," we can just use a switch/case statement on the task and look at each possible value individually.

Listing 6.7 and Applet 6.7 (at the end of this chapter) use the rock, scissors, paper game to demonstrate the switch/case statement.

To use switch/case:

1. switch(appNum) {
    case 1:
        appChoice = "Rock";
        break;
    case 2:
        appChoice = "Scissors";
        break;
    case 3:
        appChoice = "Paper";
        break;
    default:
        appChoice = "Error";
}

As in the previous examples, we use Java's random-number generator to pick whether rock, scissors, or paper is the applet's choice. Given that we have appNum, a random number between 1 and 3, the applet has to set appChoice. Here, we switch between case statements based on the number appNum. The above code can be read as "if (appNum == 1) {appChoice="Rock"} else if (appNum ==2) {appChoice="Scissors"} else if..." and so on.

2. switch (userChoice.charAt(0)) {
    case 'R':
        userNum = 1;
        break;
    case 'S':
        userNum = 2;
        break;
    case 'P':
        userNum = 3;
        break;
    default:
        userNum = 0;
}

In this segment, a char is being checked instead of a number. The user entered their choice by clicking on a radio button, which triggered an event. Java knows which radio button was pressed, and the applet here uses the first letter of the user's choice to convert that choice into a number to be compared to the applet's choice. Figure 6.15 shows how the game begins, and Figures 6.16, 6.17, and 6.18 show some of the possible outcomes.

✔ Tips

■ A switch/case statement can only be used on four primitive types: byte, char, int, and short. This is why in the second step, above, we're checking just the first character of userChoice instead of the entire string.

■ If the break is left out of any of the above case blocks, the code will fall through to the next block and execute that also. This can be a useful feature, but is also a major source of bugs. Remember to put a break at the end of each case statement!

■ If none of the values in the case statements match, the default block is executed. No matter how sure you are that your code will never execute the default, you should always include it just in case.

Figure 6.15 Ready to start the game...

Figure 6.16 The user wins the first game...

Figure 6.17 ...then a tie game...

Figure 6.18 ...and then the computer wins one.

Applet 6.7 Let's see if we can beat the Applet.

```
                    Applet

import java.awt.*;
import java.applet.Applet;
import java.awt.Font;

public class Applet7 extends Applet {
 int appNum = (int)(java.lang.Math.random()
 ⇢* 3)+1;
 Font f = new Font("TimesRoman",Font.BOLD,
 ⇢16);
 CheckboxGroup userCheckbox;
 boolean firstTime = true;
 String userChoice;

 public void init() {
   setBackground(Color.white);

   userCheckbox = new CheckboxGroup();
   add(new Checkbox("Rock",userCheckbox,false));
   add(new
   ⇢Checkbox("Scissors",userCheckbox,false));
   add(new Checkbox("Paper",userCheckbox,false));
 }

 public void paint(Graphics g) {
   int userNum;
   String appChoice;

   g.setFont(f);

   if (firstTime) {
     g.drawString("Play Rock, Scissors, Paper
     ⇢ with me!",20,60);
     firstTime = false;
   }
   else {
     switch(appNum) {
       case 1:
         appChoice = "Rock";
         break;
       case 2:
         appChoice = "Scissors";
         break;
       case 3:
         appChoice = "Paper";
         break;
       default:
         appChoice = "Error";
     }

     switch (userChoice.charAt(0)) {
       case 'R':
         userNum = 1;
         break;
       case 'S':
         userNum = 2;
         break;
       case 'P':
         userNum = 3;
         break;
       default:
```

Applet 6.7 *Continued*

```
                    Applet

       userNum = 0;
   }

   if (appNum == userNum) {
     g.drawString("Tie game—let's play again.",
     ⇢ 20, 60);
   }
   else {
     if ((userNum==1 && appNum==3) || (userNum=
     ⇢=2 && appNum==1) || (userNum==3 && appNum
     ⇢==2)) {
       g.drawString("I win! I picked
       ⇢ "+appChoice+".", 20, 60);
     }
     else {
       g.drawString("You win! I picked
       ⇢ "+appChoice+".", 20, 60);
     }
   }
   g.drawString("Reload the page to play
   ⇢ another game",20,80);
 }
}

public boolean action(Event e, Object arg) {
  if (e.target instanceof Checkbox) {
    userChoice = userCheckbox.getCurrent().
    ⇢getLabel();
    repaint();
    return true;
  }
  return false;
 }
}
```

WORKING WITH THE USER

7

One of the main goals of using Java applets is to increase how much users interact with your pages. In this chapter, we'll cover ways to let users control the actions of applets, using both the mouse and the keyboard.

Drawing with the mouse

In this example, the applet does nothing at all until the user takes an action. Consequently, everything takes place within event handlers, where the Java applet handles the events that are triggered when the user presses the mouse button, drags the mouse, and releases the button. Listing 7.1 and Applet 7.1 allow the user to draw the line.

To draw lines using the mouse:

1. public boolean mouseDown(Event evt, int x,
   → int y) {
      startPt = new Point(x, y);
      return true;
   }

   The first event we need to handle is the mouseDown() event. This is triggered whenever the user clicks the mouse within the applet's boundaries.

   When this happens, the mouseDown() method is called and passed three variables: an event and the x and y coordinates (two ints) where the user clicked the mouse.

   When this happens, we set the variable startPt to save the point where the user clicked the mouse, and return true to signify that the event was handled satisfactorily.

2. public boolean mouseDrag(Event evt, int x,
   → int y) {
      endPt = new Point(x, y);
      repaint();
      return true;
   }

   Next, we handle the mouseDrag() event. This event is triggered when the mouse is moved while the button is pressed. This method takes the same three parameters, but this time sets the variable endPt. This is the end point of the line that we want to draw, so we call the standard Java repaint() method (which will call our paint()

Listing 7.1 Putting a table with a border of 1 around an applet helps to show the applet's boundaries.

```
<HTML>
<HEAD>
 <TITLE>Listing 7.1</TITLE>
</HEAD>
<BODY BGCOLOR=WHITE>
 <TABLE BORDER=1 CELLPADDING=0
 → CELLSPACING=0><TR><TD>
 <APPLET CODEBASE="classes" CODE="Applet1.class"
 → WIDTH=500 HEIGHT=100>
 </APPLET>
 </TD></TR></TABLE>
</BODY>
</HTML>
```

Applet 7.1 This applet handles and responds to the user's mouse movements.

```
import java.awt.*;
import java.applet.*;

public class Applet1 extends Applet {
  Point startPt, endPt;

  public void init() {
     setBackground(Color.white);
  }

  public boolean mouseDown(Event evt, int x, int
 → y) {
     startPt = new Point(x, y);
     return true;
  }

  public boolean mouseDrag(Event evt, int x, int
 → y) {
     endPt = new Point(x, y);
     repaint();
     return true;
  }

  public boolean mouseUp(Event evt, int x, int y)
 → {
     endPt = new Point(x,y);
     repaint();
     return true;
  }

  public void paint(Graphics g) {
     if (endPt != null) {
        g.drawLine(startPt.x, startPt.y, endPt.x,
 → endPt.y);
     }
  }
}
```

Figure 7.1 Displaying the line that the user drew

method to force the image to be redrawn) and return true.

3. public boolean mouseUp(Event evt, int x,
→ int y) {
  endPt = new Point(x,y);
  repaint();
  return true;
}

The mouseUp() method should look very similar to the mouseDrag() method. In fact, they're identical. In both cases, we want to draw a line from the starting point to the new end point. The mouseDrag() method is probably sufficient for setting endPt, but we do it again here to be absolutely sure that the line is displayed just the way we've drawn it.

4. public void paint(Graphics g) {
    if (endPt != null) {
        g.drawLine(startPt.x, startPt.y, endPt.x,
        → endPt.y);
    }
}

In our paint() method, we actually do the line drawing, as shown in Figure 7.1. Once an end point has been set (by the mouseDown and mouseDrag events), we're ready to draw a line.

The dragLine() method takes four parameters: the x and y coordinates of the starting point and the x and y coordinates of the ending point.

✔ Tip

- You might wonder what would happen if we simply moved the drawLine() method into the mouseDrag() and mouseUp() methods, and skipped the paint() method altogether. But, behind the scenes, the paint() method is clearing the applet area before the new line is drawn. This lets you move the end point of the line around without seeing a trail of previous lines.

DRAWING WITH THE MOUSE

Drawing in two dimensions

There are many shapes that can be drawn in Java besides one-dimensional lines. Listing 7.2 and Applet 7.2 take the user's mouse movements and translate them into a two-dimensional object.

To draw an object:

1. int rectWidth, rectHeight, startX, startY;

   The only difference between this applet and the previous applet is within the paint() method, where we handle the actual drawing. This method starts by declaring four local variables: rectWidth (the width of the rectangle), rectHeight (the height of the rectangle), and startX and startY (the x and y coordinates of the top-left corner of the rectangle).

2. startX = Math.min(startPt.x,endPt.x);
   startY = Math.min(startPt.y,endPt.y);

   We start off by setting startX and startY. While a line can go in any direction, a rectangle needs to start drawing in the top-left corner. Because the user may have clicked in the lower-right corner (or upper-right or lower-left), we need to calculate the starting coordinates. The startX and startY variables are calculated by finding the lesser of the two positions, using the java.lang.Math.min() method.

3. rectWidth = Math.abs(endPt.x -startPt.x);
   rectHeight = Math.abs(endPt.y - startPt.y);

   Unlike a line, which just needs a beginning and ending point, a rectangle wants a beginning point, a width, and a height. Because where we start drawing may not be the same as startPt or endPt, the width and height need to be calculated. We do this by finding the absolute value (i.e., the positive value) of startPt's x and y coordinates subtracted from endPt's x and y

Listing 7.2 Placing an applet on a Web page

```
<HTML>
<HEAD>
 <TITLE>Listing 7.2</TITLE>
</HEAD>
<BODY BGCOLOR=WHITE>
 <TABLE BORDER=1 CELLPADDING=0
 → CELLSPACING=0><TR><TD>
 <APPLET CODEBASE="classes" CODE="Applet2.class"
 → WIDTH=500 HEIGHT=100>
 </APPLET>
 </TD></TR></TABLE>
</BODY>
</HTML>
```

Applet 7.2 Here's how to draw a rectangle on that Web page, with the user setting the dimensions via the mouse.

```
import java.awt.*;
import java.applet.*;
import java.lang.*;

public class Applet2 extends Applet {
 Point startPt, endPt;

 public void init() {
   setBackground(Color.white);
 }

 public boolean mouseDown(Event evt, int x, int
 → y) {
   startPt = new Point(x, y);
   return true;
 }

 public boolean mouseDrag(Event evt, int x, int
 → y) {
   endPt = new Point(x, y);
   repaint();
   return true;
 }

 public boolean mouseUp(Event evt, int x, int y)
 → {
   endPt = new Point(x,y);
   repaint();
   return true;
 }

 public void paint(Graphics g) {
   int rectWidth, rectHeight, startX, startY;

   if (endPt != null) {
     startX = Math.min(startPt.x,endPt.x);
     startY = Math.min(startPt.y,endPt.y);
     rectWidth = Math.abs(endPt.x - startPt.x);
     rectHeight = Math.abs(endPt.y - startPt.y);

     g.fillRect(startX, startY, rectWidth,
     → rectHeight);
   }
 }
}
```

Figure 7.2 And here's our rectangle.

Table 7.1

Drawing Methods

Method	Description	Parameters
drawRect	Draw the outline of a rectangle	startX, startY, width, height
fillRect	Draw a filled-in rectangle	startX, startY, width, height
drawRoundRect	Draw a rectangle with rounded corners	startX, startY, width, height, curveX, curveY
drawOval	Draw the outline of an oval	startX, startY, width, height
fillOval	Draw a filled-in oval	startX, startY, width, height

coordinates. The result gives the correct width and height.

4. g.fillRect(startX, startY, rectWidth,
→ rectHeight);

The fillRect() method draws a solid rectangle with the previously calculated dimensions, as shown in Figure 7.2. Table 7.1 shows some of Java's other drawing methods.

✔ Tip

■ Forcing the width and height to be the same will cause the rectangle methods to produce a square, and cause the oval methods to draw a circle.

DRAWING IN TWO DIMENSIONS

Freehand drawing

While drawing lines and boxes is interesting at first, you'll soon be looking for something a little more creative. Listing 7.3 and Applet 7.3 demonstrate how you can allow unlimited artistry within the boundaries of your applet.

To draw in your applet:

1. Graphics g = getGraphics();

   Because we're going to be handling the drawing inside the mouseDrag() method, we need to create a graphics region. Here, we're declaring g and initializing it for later use.

2. g.drawLine(startPt.x, startPt.y, endPt.x, → endPt.y);

   As in Applet 7.1, we draw a line from our starting point to our current point, as shown in Figure 7.3.

3. startPt = endPt;

   In order for this routine to work properly, startPt now needs to be reset to what we just used as endPt. In this way, our current point is now the beginning of the next line we're about to draw, and so on.

   Because we're just drawing little connected line segments, the drawing appears to follow the path of the cursor.

Listing 7.3 Places Applet 7.3 on the Web page

```
<HTML>
<HEAD>
 <TITLE>Listing 7.3</TITLE>
</HEAD>
<BODY BGCOLOR=WHITE>
 <TABLE BORDER=1 CELLPADDING=0
  → CELLSPACING=0><TR><TD>
 <APPLET CODEBASE="classes" CODE="Applet3.class"
  → WIDTH=500 HEIGHT=100>
 </APPLET>
 </TD></TR></TABLE>
</BODY>
</HTML>
```

Applet 7.3 Allows the user to draw anything they want within the applet's boundaries (and within the boundaries of the user's artistic talent).

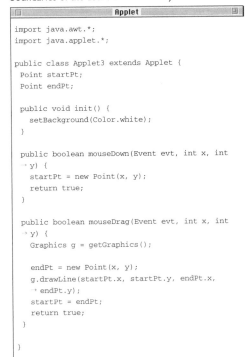

```
import java.awt.*;
import java.applet.*;

public class Applet3 extends Applet {
 Point startPt;
 Point endPt;

 public void init() {
   setBackground(Color.white);
 }

 public boolean mouseDown(Event evt, int x, int
  → y) {
   startPt = new Point(x, y);
   return true;
 }

 public boolean mouseDrag(Event evt, int x, int
  → y) {
   Graphics g = getGraphics();

   endPt = new Point(x, y);
   g.drawLine(startPt.x, startPt.y, endPt.x,
    → endPt.y);
   startPt = endPt;
   return true;
 }

}
```

Figure 7.3 Hey, this was fun!

FREEHAND DRAWING

Listing 7.4 This HTML displays Applet 7.4.

```
                    Listing

<HTML>
<HEAD>
 <TITLE>Listing 7.4</TITLE>
</HEAD>
<BODY BGCOLOR=WHITE>
 <TABLE BORDER=1 CELLPADDING=0
 → CELLSPACING=0><TR><TD>
 <APPLET CODEBASE="classes" CODE="Applet4.class"
 → WIDTH=500 HEIGHT=100>
 </APPLET>
 </TD></TR></TABLE>
</BODY>
</HTML>
```

Applet 7.4 Here's where we grab the pressed key and display it on the Web page…

```
                    Applet

import java.awt.*;
import java.applet.*;

public class Applet4 extends Applet {
 char currentChar = ' ';

 public void init() {
   setBackground(Color.white);
   setFont(new Font("Times Roman",Font.BOLD,36));
 }

 public boolean keyDown(Event evt, int x) {
   currentChar = (char)x;
   repaint();
   return true;
 }

 public void paint(Graphics g) {
   g.drawString(String.valueOf(currentChar),
   →200,50);
 }
}
```

Figure 7.4 …and here's the end result.

Capturing keystrokes

Working with the mouse is fun, but there's an entire keyboard to work with, too. Listing 7.4 and Applet 7.4 capture the keystrokes entered by the user and display them on the Web page.

To capture keystrokes:

1. public boolean keyDown(Event evt, nt x) {
    currentChar = (char)x;
    repaint();
    return true;
}

Whenever a key is pressed on the keyboard, the keyDown() method is triggered. The parameters to keydown() are the event and the ASCII value of the key pressed.

In this method, we're setting currentChar to the key pressed, by casting (i.e., converting) the value of x to a char. The method then calls repaint() and returns true to signify that the keydown action has been successfully handled.

2. public void paint(Graphics g) {
    g.drawString(String.valueOf(currentChar),
    → 200, 50);
}

The paint() method takes the value of currentChar, turns it into a string, and uses the drawString() method to display the pressed key at position (200,50). The result is shown in Figure 7.4.

Moving images around

Okay, we've seen how to show the user what key they just pressed. But then again, the user knows what key they pressed—they're the one who pressed it, right?

In this example, we'll let the user press the arrow keys to move an image around the page. The butterfly will move in any direction that the user tells it to fly, as shown in Listing 7.5 and Applet 7.5.

To move an image using the arrow keys:

1. public boolean keyDown(Event evt, int x) {
　　switch (x) {
　　　　case (Event.UP):
　　　　　　yPos -= 10;
　　　　　　break;
　　　　case (Event.DOWN):
　　　　　　yPos += 10;
　　　　　　break;
　　　　case (Event.LEFT):
　　　　　　xPos -= 10;
　　　　　　break;
　　　　case (Event.RIGHT):
　　　　　　xPos += 10;
　　　　　　break;
　　}

The keydown() method is passed the ASCII value of the pressed key, so we can use that key in a switch statement (as defined in Chapter 6) to choose how to handle each arrow key. Each arrow key corresponds to one of the four Event directions: Event.UP, Event.DOWN, Event.LEFT, and Event.RIGHT. If the Up Arrow is pressed, the applet subtracts 10 from the butterfly's y coordinate. If the Down Arrow is pressed, 10 is added to the y coordinate. The Left and Right Arrows subtract and add 10 (respectively) to the x coordinate.

Listing 7.5 Setting up the butterfly applet.

```
<HTML>
<HEAD>
 <TITLE>Listing 7.5</TITLE>
</HEAD>
<BODY BGCOLOR=WHITE>
 <TABLE BORDER=1 CELLPADDING=0
 → CELLSPACING=0><TR><TD>
 <APPLET CODEBASE="classes" CODE="Applet5.class"
 → WIDTH=500 HEIGHT=100>
 </APPLET>
 </TD></TR></TABLE>
</BODY>
</HTML>
```

Applet 7.5 Using the arrow keys to control the butterfly's direction.

```
import java.awt.*;
import java.applet.*;

public class Applet5 extends Applet {
 int xPos, yPos;
 Image butterfly;

 public void init() {
   setBackground(Color.white);
   xPos = 100;
   yPos = 50;
   butterfly = getImage(getCodeBase(),
   →"butterfly.gif");
 }

 public boolean keyDown(Event evt, int x) {
   switch (x) {
     case (Event.UP):
       yPos -= 10;
       break;
     case (Event.DOWN):
       yPos += 10;
       break;
     case (Event.LEFT):
       xPos -= 10;
       break;
     case (Event.RIGHT):
       xPos += 10;
       break;
   }
   repaint();
   return true;
 }

 public void paint(Graphics g) {
   g.drawImage(butterfly,xPos,yPos,this);
 }
}
```

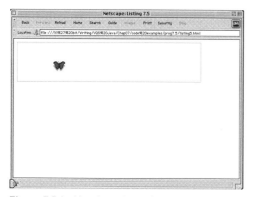

Figure 7.5 And here's our butterfly .

2. repaint();
return true;

Once the new position of the image has been calculated, we call repaint() to force the image to be redrawn in its new position, and return true to tell Java that the keydown event has been successfully handled.

3. public void paint(Graphics g) {
    g.drawImage(butterfly,xPos,yPos,this);
}

We end by calling the paint() method to display the butterfly gliding around the window, as shown in Figure 7.5.

✔ Tip

■ If you move the butterfly both horizontally and vertically (e.g. left and up) almost simultaneously, its movement appears very realistic.

MOVING IMAGES AROUND

Using modifier keys

To make the butterfly's motion truly realistic, we need to be able to move it at different speeds. In this example, holding down the Shift key doubles the speed (in any direction) that the butterfly travels. Listing 7.6 and Applet 7.6 show how this is accomplished.

To use modifier keys to change an action:

1. if (evt.shiftDown()) {
       offset = 20;
   }
   else {
       offset = 10;
   }

   Within the keyDown() method, we can check to see if a modifier key (or keys) was held down. In this case, we're checking to see if the Shift key was held down when the arrow key was pressed.

   If so, we set the variable offset to 20; if not, it's set to 10. This variable is then used to change the x and y coordinates of the image. Obviously, if the variable is set to 20, the butterfly moves twice as fast. Figure 7.6 shows the applet in action.

Listing 7.6 This HTML places Applet 7.6 on the page.

```
<HTML>
<HEAD>
 <TITLE>Listing 7.6</TITLE>
</HEAD>
<BODY BGCOLOR=WHITE>
 <TABLE BORDER=1 CELLPADDING=0
 → CELLSPACING=0><TR><TD>
 <APPLET CODEBASE="classes" CODE="Applet6.class"
 → WIDTH=500 HEIGHT=100>
 </APPLET>
 </TD></TR></TABLE>
</BODY>
</HTML>
```

Applet 7.6 The new and improved butterfly applet

```
import java.awt.*;
import java.applet.*;

public class Applet6 extends Applet {
 int xPos, yPos;
 Image butterfly;

 public void init() {
    setBackground(Color.white);
    xPos = this.size().width/2;
    yPos = this.size().height/2;
    butterfly =
    → getImage(getCodeBase(),"butterfly.gif");
 }

 public boolean keyDown(Event evt, int x) {
    int offset;

    if (evt.shiftDown()) {
       offset = 20;
    }
    else {
       offset = 10;
    }

    switch (x) {
       case (Event.UP):
          yPos -= offset;
          break;
       case (Event.DOWN):
          yPos += offset;
          break;
       case (Event.LEFT):
          xPos -= offset;
          break;
       case (Event.RIGHT):
          xPos += offset;
          break;
    }
    repaint();
    return true;
 }

 public void paint(Graphics g) {
    g.drawImage(butterfly,xPos,yPos,this);
 }
}
```

Figure 7.6 And here's the version 2 butterfly, happily winging around the Web.

✔ Tip

■ In the previous example, the initial values of xPos and yPos were hard-coded, that is, set once and never changed. There's no way of knowing that those would be valid values, so it's better to calculate the placement on the fly (so to speak). In this example, this.size().width and this.size().height are the dimensions of the applet boundary. Dividing each of these numbers by two puts the image in the direct center of the applet.

BUILDING A
USER INTERFACE

One of the main reasons for adding a Java applet to your page is to interact with the user. In order to interact with a user, you'll need to have a *user interface*: fields into which the user can enter data, checkboxes and radio buttons for them to click, and so on.

This chapter covers the most common user-interface elements and how to add each to your applet.

Password-protecting a page

It's very common to want to protect one page or one area of your Web site from the eyes of random surfers. Listing 8.1 and Applet 8.1 show a simple Java applet that requests a password. If the correct password is entered, the protected page is then loaded.

To password-protect a page:

1. try {
       passwordURL = new URL("http://www.
       → chalcedony.com/java/");
   }
   catch (MalformedURLException err) {
       passwordURL = this.getDocumentBase();
   }

   First, we create a new URL variable, and assign it the URL that we want to load if the correct password is entered. Here, the URL we want to go to is http://www. → chalcedony.com/java. The try/catch is required, just in case the URL we're using isn't in a valid format, which would then trigger the MalformedURLException error (for more about try/catch, see Chapter 6). In that case, we would set the URL to be that of the current page.

2. add(new Label("Password"));
   passwordField = new TextField(10);
   passwordField.setEchoCharacter('*');
   add(passwordField);

   The first line adds the label "Password" to the screen. Then, we create a text-entry field with a length of 10 named passwordField, which will echo asterisks (*) when text is typed into the field, and add it to the screen as shown in Figure 8.2.

3. if (badPass) {
       g.drawString("Incorrect Password—try
       → again",200,40);

Listing 8.1 This HTML file calls Applet 8.1.

```
<HTML>
<HEAD>
 <TITLE>Listing 8.1</TITLE>
</HEAD>
<BODY BGCOLOR=WHITE>
 <APPLET CODEBASE="classes" CODE="Applet1.class"
 → WIDTH=500 HEIGHT=300>
 </APPLET>
</BODY>
</HTML>
```

Figure 8.1 Enter the password here.

Figure 8.2 If the correct password wasn't entered, the error message is displayed.

✔ Tip

■ It's possible to guess what the correct value of the password is by looking at the applet's .class file. To protect against this, you can either add a bunch of dummy strings to your applet or piece together the target password by concatenating several strings.

Applet 8.1 This applet protects the following page by requiring the correct password.

```
                      Applet
import java.awt.*;
import java.applet.Applet;
import java.net.*;

public class Applet1 extends Applet {
 TextField passwordField;
 boolean badPass = false;
 URL passwordURL;

 public void init() {
   setBackground(Color.white);

   try {
     passwordURL =
     → newURL("http://www.chalcedony.com/java/");
   }
   catch (MalformedURLException err) {
     passwordURL = this.getDocumentBase();
   }

   add(new Label("Password"));
   passwordField = new TextField(10);
   passwordField.setEchoCharacter('*');
   add(passwordField);
 }

 public void paint(Graphics g) {
   if (badPass) {
     g.drawString("Incorrect Password—try again",
     → 200,40);
   }
 }

 public boolean action(Event e, Object arg) {
   if (e.target instanceof TextField) {
     if (passwordField.getText().equals
     → ("peachpit")) {
       getAppletContext().showDocument(password
       → URL);
     }
     else {
       badPass = true;
       repaint();
     }
     return true;
   }
   return false;
 }
}
```

If the bad password flag has been set (done in step 5), the line "Incorrect Password—try again" is displayed, as shown in Figure 8.2 on the previous page.

4. if (e.target instanceof TextField) {
  if (passwordField.getText().equals
  → ("peachpit")) {   getAppletContext().showDocument
  → (passwordURL);
  }

There are many possible actions that could be triggered, even in an applet this small. In this case, the only event we care about is when a user has finished entering data into the text field **passwordField**. Once they're finished, the applet gets the entered data by calling **getText()**, and compares it to the password we're checking against, in this case "peachpit". If the values are equal, **showDocument()** is called to load the new URL into the browser window.

5.   else {
       badPass = true;
       repaint();
     }
     return true;
   }
   return false;

If the password attempt failed, we set the bad password flag to **true** and repaint the applet. If we've finished handling a TextField, **true** is returned to show that no more handling needs to be done. If the event was anything else, **false** is returned to signify that the event wasn't handled here.

Entering and displaying text

Java allows you to both enter text into a field and display text on the screen. In Listing 8.2 and Applet 8.2, whatever you enter into the field is then displayed again by the applet.

To enter and display text:

1. TextField inputField;
   String displayText = "Enter a string to
   → display";

   Two new variables are declared here, inputField (of type TextField) and display-Text (of type String). The latter is initialized to the value "Enter a string to display." The first time the applet paints the screen, this is the text that will appear.

2. add(new Label("Text String:"));
   inputField = new TextField(25);
   add(inputField);

   These lines add the label "Text String:" to the screen, as well as a new text-entry field of length 25.

3. g.drawString(displayText,200,40);

   This line within the paint() method uses drawString() to display the value of display-Text on the screen. When it's first run, the value is "Enter a string to display," as shown in Figure 8.3. After that, whatever the user has entered is displayed, as shown in Figure 8.4.

4. displayText = inputField.getText();
   repaint();
   return true;

   This code is executed when the event being handled is the user leaving the text field. In this case, we get the value of inputField with the method getText(), repaint the screen, and return true to show that the event has been handled.

Listing 8.2 This calls Applet 8.2.

```
<HTML>
<HEAD>
 <TITLE>Listing 8.2</TITLE>
</HEAD>
<BODY BGCOLOR=WHITE>
 <APPLET CODEBASE="classes" CODE="Applet2.class"
 → WIDTH=500 HEIGHT=300>
 </APPLET>
</BODY>
</HTML>
```

Applet 8.2 This applet allows a user to enter a string, which will then be displayed on the screen.

```
import java.awt.*;
import java.applet.Applet;

public class Applet2 extends Applet {
  TextField inputField;
  String displayText = "Enter a string to
  → display";

  public void init() {
    setBackground(Color.white);

    add(new Label("Text String:"));
    inputField = new TextField(25);
    add(inputField);
  }

  public void paint(Graphics g) {
    g.drawString(displayText,200,40);
  }

  public boolean action(Event e, Object arg) {
    if (e.target instanceof TextField) {
      displayText = inputField.getText();
      repaint();
      return true;
    }
    return false;
  }
}
```

Figure 8.3 Here's what the applet looks like at the beginning...

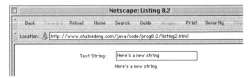

Figure 8.4 ...and here's what it looks like after something's been entered.

Listing 8.3 Calls Applet 8.3

```
                    Listing
<HTML>
<HEAD>
 <TITLE>Listing 8.3</TITLE>
</HEAD>
<BODY BGCOLOR=WHITE>
 <APPLET CODEBASE="classes" CODE="Applet3.class"
 → WIDTH=500 HEIGHT=300>
 </APPLET>
</BODY>
</HTML>
```

Applet 8.3 A text-entry field and two checkboxes allow a string to be entered and displayed in four different styles.

```
                    Applet
import java.awt.*;
import java.applet.Applet;

public class Applet3 extends Applet {
 TextField inputField;
 String displayText = "Enter a string to display";
 int fontStyle = Font.PLAIN;

 public void init() {
   setBackground(Color.white);

   add(new Label("Text String:"));
   inputField = new TextField(25);
   add(inputField);

   add(new Label("Font Style:"));
   add(new Checkbox("Bold",null,false));
   add(new Checkbox("Italic",null,false));
 }

 public void paint(Graphics g) {
   g.setFont(new Font("TimesRoman",fontStyle,24));
   g.drawString(displayText,200,60);
 }

 public boolean action(Event e, Object arg) {
   Checkbox boxLabel;

   if (e.target instanceof TextField) {
     displayText = inputField.getText();
     repaint();
     return true;
   }
   if (e.target instanceof Checkbox) {
     boxLabel = (Checkbox) e.target;

     if (boxLabel.getLabel() == "Bold") {
       if (boxLabel.getState()) {
         fontStyle += Font.BOLD;
       }
       else {
         fontStyle -= Font.BOLD;
       }
     }

     if (boxLabel.getLabel() == "Italic") {
       if (boxLabel.getState()) {
         fontStyle += Font.ITALIC;
       }
       else {
       fontStyle -= Font.ITALIC;
       }
     }
     repaint();
     return true;
   }
   return false;
 }
}
```

Working with checkboxes

One of the most common user-interface elements is the checkbox. This is an on/off field, where the box is either checked or not checked. In Listing 8.3 and Applet 8.3, checkboxes are used to allow the user to pick the style of the displayed text.

To work with checkboxes:

1. add(new Checkbox("Bold",null,false));
add(new Checkbox("Italic",null,false));

This code adds two new checkboxes to the applet, one labeled "Bold" and the other labeled "Italic." The second parameter of Checkbox identifies whether a new checkbox is actually a radio button; in this case, they aren't, so the second parameter is null. The third parameter gives the initial value for each checkbox, which we've set to false so neither box starts off checked.

2. if (e.target instanceof Checkbox) {
boxLabel = (Checkbox) e.target;

Here's where we start to handle checkbox events. The target of the event was a checkbox, so we cast the target as a checkbox and call that variable boxLabel for later use.

3. if (boxLabel.getLabel() == "Bold") {
if (boxLabel.getState()) {
fontStyle += Font.BOLD;
}
else {
fontStyle -= Font.BOLD;
}
}

Here, we first check to see which checkbox the user clicked. In this case, the method getLabel() shows that we're working on "Bold." The method getState() returns the new value of the checkbox that the user has just toggled. If the value is true, the

WORKING WITH CHECKBOXES

85

value of Font.BOLD is added to fontStyle; otherwise, Font.BOLD is subtracted.

4. if (boxLabel.getLabel() == "Italic") {
    if (boxLabel.getState()) {
        fontStyle += Font.ITALIC;
    }
    else {
        fontStyle -= Font.ITALIC;
    }
}

In this case, we do the same thing, except that the user clicked on "Italic." If the new value is true, Font.ITALIC is added to the current font; otherwise, Font.ITALIC is subtracted.

✔ Tip

■ How does Java change the font style just by adding and/or subtracting a variable? Internally, Java keeps three variables: Font.PLAIN (which has an internal value of 0), Font.BOLD (with a value of 1), and Font.ITALIC (with a value of 2). The variable fontStyle is therefore initialized above to be zero, as in Figure 8.5. If the user checks "Bold," fontStyle is set to 1, as in Figure 8.6. If the user then checks "Italic," fontStyle becomes 3, as in Figure 8.7. If the user then unchecks "Bold," fontStyle is 2, as in Figure 8.8.

Figure 8.5 This is what is displayed when the applet is loaded.

Figure 8.6 When the "Bold" checkbox is checked, the string is displayed in bold text.

Figure 8.7 If "Italic" is then checked, the display is both bold and italic.

Figure 8.8 If "Bold" is subsequently unchecked, the string is displayed as italic only.

Listing 8.4 Calls Applet 8.4

```
<HTML>
<HEAD>
 <TITLE>Listing 8.4</TITLE>
</HEAD>
<BODY BGCOLOR=WHITE>
 <APPLET CODEBASE="classes" CODE="Applet4.class"
 → WIDTH=500 HEIGHT=300>
 </APPLET>
</BODY>
</HTML>
```

Figure 8.9 This font is too small...

Figure 8.10 ...this font is too large...

Figure 8.11 ...but this font size is just right.

Using radio buttons

Radio buttons are a special type of checkbox, where only one of the group may be selected at any one time. When a user clicks on one of the buttons, Java handles turning all the others off. Listing 8.4 and Applet 8.4 (on the next page) use radio buttons to allow the user to pick a font size.

To use radio buttons:

1. fontSizeField = new CheckboxGroup();
   add(new Checkbox("12", fontSizeField, true));
   add(new Checkbox("14", fontSizeField, false));
   add(new Checkbox("18", fontSizeField, false));
   add(new Checkbox("24", fontSizeField, false));

   This code, inside init(), creates the four radio buttons that control the font size of the displayed string. The variable font-SizeField is a CheckboxGroup, and using this as the second parameter to Checkbox identifies the new fields as part of the same radio button set. The radio button with the label "12" is initialized to be on by setting the third parameter to true.

2. fontSize = Integer.parseInt
　→ (fontSizeField.getCurrent().getLabel());

Inside the event handler, we can find out the new font size with one complex line of code. The easiest way to understand this line is by working from the inside out. Given that we know that we're working on the radio button set called fontSizeField, we can ask Java to return the radio button that's currently on, using the method getCurrent(). Given that, Java can return the label of that radio button, which returns the current font size as a string. Integer.parseInt() takes that string and turns it into an integer, which is our new value for fontSize.

Applet 8.4 This applet demonstrates how radio buttons are used; in this case, they let the user choose the font size.

```
Applet
import java.awt.*;
import java.applet.Applet;

public class Applet4 extends Applet {
  TextField inputField;
  String displayText = "Enter a string to
→display";
  int fontSize = 12;
  CheckboxGroup  fontSizeField;


  public void init() {
    setBackground(Color.white);

    add(new Label("Text String:"));
    inputField = new TextField(20);
    add(inputField);

    add(new Label("Font Size:"));
    fontSizeField = new CheckboxGroup();
    add(new Checkbox("12",fontSizeField,true));
    add(new Checkbox("14",fontSizeField,false));
    add(new Checkbox("18",fontSizeField,false));
    add(new Checkbox("24",fontSizeField,false));
  }

  public void paint(Graphics g) {
    g.setFont(new Font("TimesRoman",Font.PLAIN,
→fontSize));
    g.drawString(displayText,200,60);
  }

  public boolean action(Event e, Object arg) {
    if (e.target instanceof TextField) {
      displayText = inputField.getText();
      repaint();
      return true;
    }
    if (e.target instanceof Checkbox) {
      fontSize = Integer.parseInt(
→fontSizeField.getCurrent().getLabel());
      repaint();
      return true;
    }
    return false;
  }
}
```

Listing 8.5 Calls Applet 8.5

```
                     Listing
<HTML>
<HEAD>
 <TITLE>Listing 8.5</TITLE>
</HEAD>
<BODY BGCOLOR=WHITE>
 <APPLET CODEBASE="classes" CODE="Applet5.class"
 → WIDTH=500 HEIGHT=300>
 </APPLET>
</BODY>
</HTML>
```

Applet 8.5 Sets up the new pull-down menu to allow the user to pick the font of their choice

```
                     Applet
import java.awt.*;
import java.applet.Applet;

public class Applet5 extends Applet {
  TextField inputField;
  String displayText = "Enter a string to display";
  String fontFace = "TimesRoman";
  Choice fontMenu;

  public void init() {
    setBackground(Color.white);

    add(new Label("Text String:"));
    inputField = new TextField(20);
    add(inputField);

    fontMenu = new Choice();
    fontMenu.addItem("TimesRoman");
    fontMenu.addItem("Helvetica");
    fontMenu.addItem("Courier");
    fontMenu.addItem("Dialog");
    fontMenu.addItem("DialogInput");
    add(fontMenu);
  }

  public void paint(Graphics g) {
    g.setFont(new Font(fontFace,Font.PLAIN,24));
    g.drawString(displayText,150,60);
  }

  public boolean action(Event e, Object arg) {
    if (e.target instanceof TextField) {
      displayText = inputField.getText();
      repaint();
      return true;
    }
    if (e.target instanceof Choice) {
      fontFace = (String) arg;
      repaint();
      return true;
    }
    return false;
  }
}
```

Selecting menu items

Pull-down menus give us another way to permit only one of a group of items to be chosen. Listing 8.5 and Applet 8.5 use a pull-down menu to allow the user to choose which font a message is displayed in.

To use a pull-down menu:

1. fontMenu = new Choice();
   fontMenu.addItem("TimesRoman");
   fontMenu.addItem("Helvetica");
   fontMenu.addItem("Courier");
   fontMenu.addItem("Dialog");
   fontMenu.addItem("DialogInput");
   add(fontMenu);

   We start by declaring a new variable, font-Menu, of type Choice. Once we have this new variable, we can add menu items by calling addItem. The entire menu is then added to the screen by doing an add() of fontMenu.

2. if (e.target instanceof Choice) {
       fontFace = (String) arg;
       repaint();
       return true;
   }

   If the event was an instance of Choice, we need to handle the new font face. Simply casting arg as a String gives us whichever menu option the user chose.

Figure 8.12 One view of how this applet appears, in this case using Netscape on a Mac

Figure 8.13 The same applet, but viewed using Internet Explorer on a PC

Using Java to set up the font menu

In the previous example, we set the list of fonts in the menu to be five hard-coded fonts that we expected Java to allow. Given that Java works on many different platforms with different setups, it makes much more sense to allow Java to query itself, calculate which fonts it supports, and then add them to a font menu. Listing 8.6 and Applet 8.6 demonstrate how this is done.

To calculate a font menu:

1. String[]fontArray = Toolkit.getDefaultToolkit
   → ().getFontList();

   First, we declare a string array called fontArray, which will be set to a list of fonts that Java supports. We then get the fonts by calling the built-in Java method getFontList().

2. for (int i = 0; i < fontArray.length; i++) {
       fontMenu.addItem(fontArray[i]);
   }
   add(fontMenu);

   For each font name in fontArray, we add a menu item to fontMenu. Figures 8.14 and 8.15 show the results of this on two different platforms.

3. fontFace = fontArray[0];

   The initial value of the fontFace variable can't be hard-coded (set to a fixed value), as we don't know what fonts Java might find. As a solution, here we initialize font-Face to be whatever font Java found first.

Listing 8.6 Calls Applet 8.6

```
<HTML>
<HEAD>
 <TITLE>Listing 8.6</TITLE>
</HEAD>
<BODY BGCOLOR=WHITE>
 <APPLET CODEBASE="classes" CODE="Applet6.class"
 → WIDTH=500 HEIGHT=300>
 </APPLET>
</BODY>
</HTML>
```

Figure 8.14 The results of this applet on a Mac with Netscape 4

Figure 8.15 The results of this applet on a PC with MSIE 4

Applet 8.6 Calculates and sets up the pull-down menu of fonts

```
                      Applet
import java.awt.*;
import java.applet.Applet;

public class Applet6 extends Applet {
 TextField inputField;
 String displayText = "Enter a string to
→ display";
 String fontFace;
 Choice fontMenu;

 public void init() {
   setBackground(Color.white);

   add(new Label("Text String:"));
   inputField = new TextField(20);
   add(inputField);

   fontMenu = new Choice();
   String[] fontArray = Toolkit.getDefault
   →Toolkit().getFontList();
   for (int i = 0; i < fontArray.length; i++) {
     fontMenu.addItem(fontArray[i]);
   }
   add(fontMenu);
   fontFace = fontArray[0];
 }

 public void paint(Graphics g) {
   g.setFont(new Font(fontFace,Font.PLAIN,24));
   g.drawString(displayText,150,60);
 }

 public boolean action(Event e, Object arg) {
   if (e.target instanceof TextField) {
     displayText = inputField.getText();
     repaint();
     return true;
   }
   if (e.target instanceof Choice) {
     fontFace = (String) arg;
     repaint();
     return true;
   }
   return false;
 }
}
```

✔ Tip

■ Wondering where the "toolkit" came from in step 1? At the beginning of this book, I said that AWT stands for "Abstract Window Toolkit." Yep, we've had this toolkit with us the whole time; this is just the first time that we're referencing it by that name.

Using text areas and buttons

Two more common user-interface elements are text areas and buttons. Text areas are like text fields, but larger—they allow users to enter more than one line. Consequently, the way we've indicated in previous examples that we're done with text field data entry won't work with text areas. One solution to this is to use a button to tell the applet to check the text area for a changed value.

To use text areas and buttons:

1. inputField = new TextArea(4,25);
   add(inputField);

   These lines create a new TextArea named inputField, 4 lines high by 25 characters wide, which is then added to the screen.

2. updateButton = new Button("Update Text");
   add(updateButton);

   This creates a new button named update-Button, containing the string "Update Text," and adds it to the screen.

Listing 8.7 Calls Applet 8.7

```
<HTML>
<HEAD>
 <TITLE>Listing 8.7</TITLE>
</HEAD>
<BODY BGCOLOR=WHITE>
 <APPLET CODEBASE="classes" CODE="Applet7.class"
 → WIDTH=500 HEIGHT=300>
 </APPLET>
</BODY>
</HTML>
```

Figure 8.16 Here's how it looks on one platform...

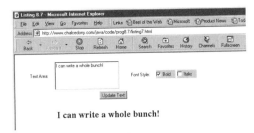

Figure 8.17 ...and on another.

Applet 8.7 We use a text area box and a button to allow the user to enter a long string to display.

```
                      Applet
import java.awt.*;
import java.applet.Applet;

public class Applet7 extends Applet {
 TextArea inputField;
 String displayText = "Enter a string to
 → display";
 int fontStyle = Font.PLAIN;
 Button updateButton;

 public void init() {
   setBackground(Color.white);

   add(new Label("Text Area:"));
   inputField = new TextArea(4,25);
   add(inputField);

   add(new Label("Font Style:"));
   add(new Checkbox("Bold",null,false));
   add(new Checkbox("Italic",null,false));

   updateButton = new Button("Update Text");
   add(updateButton);
 }

 public void paint(Graphics g) {
   g.setFont(new Font("TimesRoman",fontStyle,
   →24));
   g.drawString(displayText,100,150);
 }

 public boolean action(Event e, Object arg) {
   Checkbox   boxLabel;

   if (e.target instanceof Button) {
     displayText = inputField.getText();
     repaint();
     return true;
   }
   if (e.target instanceof Checkbox) {
     boxLabel = (Checkbox) e.target;

     if (boxLabel.getLabel() == "Bold") {
       if (boxLabel.getState()) {
         fontStyle += Font.BOLD;
       }
       else {
         fontStyle -= Font.BOLD;
       }
     }

     if (boxLabel.getLabel() == "Italic") {
       if (boxLabel.getState()) {
         fontStyle += Font.ITALIC;
       }
       else {
         fontStyle -= Font.ITALIC;
       }
     }
     repaint();
     return true;
   }
   return false;
 }
}
```

3.
```
if (e.target instanceof Button) {
    displayText = inputField.getText();
    repaint();
    return true;
}
```
If the event was triggered by a button, these lines reset the displayed text to whatever is currently in inputField and redisplay the screen. The result of this is shown in Figures 8.16 and 8.17.

Using scrolling lists

The final type of user-interface component we'll look at is the scrolling list. With a scrolling list, a user can choose any number of options from a long list, as demonstrated in Listing 8.8 and Applet 8.8.

To use a scrolling list:

1. firstList = new List(3,true);

This line creates a new scrolling list named firstList. The first parameter says that the list will display three items on the screen, no matter how many items may actually be in the list. The second parameter says that it's acceptable for someone to choose more than one item from the list. If this was set to false, the list would act like a group of radio buttons, and choosing one item would turn all the others off.

2. firstList.addItem("London");
firstList.addItem("Paris");
firstList.addItem("Rome");
firstList.addItem("Detroit");
firstList.addItem("New York");
add(firstList);

Five cities are added to the list, and the list is then added to the screen.

3. secondList = new List(3,true);
add(secondList);

A new, empty list is now added, named secondList.

4. public boolean handleEvent(Event e) {
String[] addItems;
if (e.id == Event.LIST_SELECT || e.id ==
→ Event.LIST_DESELECT) {

Scrolling lists use a different event handler than the other user-interface components we have covered in this chapter. In this case, we need to see if the mouse click caused either a LIST_SELECT or LIST_DESELECT event to take place. If so, we'll handle it here.

Listing 8.8 Calls Applet 8.8

```
Listing
<HTML>
<HEAD>
 <TITLE>Listing 8.8</TITLE>
</HEAD>
<BODY BGCOLOR=WHITE>
 <APPLET CODEBASE="classes" CODE="Applet8.class"
 → WIDTH=500 HEIGHT=300>
 </APPLET>
</BODY>
</HTML>
```

Applet 8.8 How to handle two scrolling lists

```
Applet
import java.awt.*;
import java.applet.Applet;

public class Applet8 extends Applet {
 List firstList, secondList;

 public void init() {
    setBackground(Color.white);

    firstList = new List(3,true);
    add(new Label("Please choose from the
    → following:"));
    firstList.addItem("London");
    firstList.addItem("Paris");
    firstList.addItem("Rome");
    firstList.addItem("Detroit");
    firstList.addItem("New York");
    add(firstList);

    secondList = new List(3,true);
    add(secondList);
 }

 public boolean handleEvent(Event e) {
    String[] addItems;

    if (e.id == Event.LIST_SELECT || e.id ==
    → Event.LIST_DESELECT) {
       addItems = firstList.getSelectedItems();
       secondList.clear();
       for (int i=0; i<addItems.length; i++) {
          secondList.addItem(addItems[i]);
       }
       repaint();
       return true;
    }
    return super.handleEvent(e);
 }
}
```

Figure 8.18 Should I go to London, Paris, or New York?

Figure 8.19 Or should I go to Rome or New York?

5. addItems = firstList.getSelectedItems();
   secondList.clear();
   for (int i=0; i<addItems.length; i++) {
       secondList.addItem(addItems[i]);
   }
   repaint();
   return true;

   This applet takes the items that the user has chosen in the first list and displays them in the second list.

   Whenever an item is selected or deselected in the first list, this code gets a list of all of firstList's selected items and stores it in the addItems string array. Next, secondList is emptied and then rebuilt with the list from addItems. Figures 8.18 and 8.19 show the results of the author trying to decide on a destination for her next vacation.

6. return super.handleEvent(e);

   Given the previous examples, you'd think that you could return false here and Java would pass the event on to whatever routine should handle it. In the case of a handleEvent() action, though, Java needs to be told to pass this event back through higher-level handlers. This is accomplished by calling the built-in handleEvent() method that this one has overrode, by using the super keyword.

✔ Tip

- You might notice that while the applet says to display three lines on the screen, the Mac version of the applet (Figure 8.18) actually displays four. On the Mac, one more than you've requested may be displayed.

LOOKING AT LAYOUT

You may have noticed in the previous chapters that user-interface elements decide for themselves where they want to appear in the browser window. In this chapter, we'll see how you can take charge of your interface using Java's LayoutManagers.

No layout is FlowLayout

If no LayoutManager is specified, Java assumes that you want to use the simplest Layout-Manager, called FlowLayout. Listing 9.1 and Applet 9.1 create a bunch of buttons that just "flow" where they want to.

To use FlowLayout implicitly:

1. buttonText = spaces.substring(1,i) + "Button
→ #" + i + spaces.substring(1,i);
this.add(new Button(buttonText));

This code draws ten buttons on the screen, as shown in Figures 9.1 and 9.2. Because no LayoutManager has been set, the buttons are displayed centered in the applet area.

✔ Tip

■ To make it more obvious how the example works, an increasing number of spaces is added to each button. This causes the buttons to be varying sizes.

Listing 9.1 Displays the applet in the browser window

```
<HTML>
<HEAD>
 <TITLE>Listing 9.1</TITLE>
</HEAD>
<BODY BGCOLOR=WHITE>
 <APPLET CODEBASE="classes" CODE="Applet1.class"
 → WIDTH=400 HEIGHT=100>
 </APPLET>
</BODY>
</HTML>
```

Applet 9.1 Throws ten buttons of different sizes onto the window

```
import java.awt.*;
import java.applet.*;

public class Applet1 extends Applet {

 public void init() {
  String spaces = "          ",buttonText;

  setBackground(Color.white);

  for (int i=1; i<=10; i++) {
   buttonText = spaces.substring(1,i) +
   → "Button #" + i + spaces.substring(1,i);
   this.add(new Button(buttonText));
  }
 }

}
```

Figure 9.1 This is how this applet looks on a Macintosh...

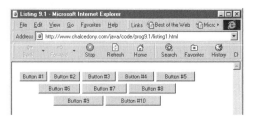

Figure 9.2 ...and it looks very similar on a PC.

Listing 9.2. This HTML file calls the Java applet.

```
                          Listing
<HTML>
<HEAD>
 <TITLE>Listing 9.2</TITLE>
</HEAD>
<BODY BGCOLOR=WHITE>
 <APPLET CODEBASE="classes" CODE="Applet2.class"
 → WIDTH=400 HEIGHT=100>
 </APPLET>
</BODY>
</HTML>
```

Applet 9.2 Here's how to make the buttons align
themselves on the left.

```
                          Applet
import java.awt.*;
import java.applet.*;

public class Applet2 extends Applet {

 public void init() {
   String spaces = "           ",buttonText;

   setBackground(Color.white);

   this.setLayout(new FlowLayout
   → (FlowLayout.LEFT));
   for (int i=1; i<=10; i++) {
     buttonText = spaces.substring(1,i) +
     → "Button #" + i + spaces.substring(1,i);
     this.add(new Button(buttonText));
   }
 }

}
```

Figure 9.3 The same buttons on the Mac, now aligned
on the left

Figure 9.4 The same buttons, aligned on the left in
Windows

Using FlowLayout

Alternatively, the layout can be explicitly set
to use FlowLayout, which gives the applet a little more control over how its components are
displayed. Listing 9.2 and Applet 9.2
provide an example of an applet where the
user-interface elements are left-aligned.

To use FlowLayout explicitly:

1. this.setLayout(new FlowLayout
    → (FlowLayout.LEFT));

    The easiest way to understand this line is
    to start from the innermost parentheses
    and work our way out. FlowLayout.LEFT is a
    Java-defined constant that tells the applet
    to display the applet left-aligned.
    Alternatively, we could have used
    FlowLayout.RIGHT or FlowLayout.CENTER.

    The alignment constant is passed to a
    class, FlowLayout. A new instance of this
    class is created (via the keyword new) and
    is passed to this.setLayout, which defines
    the LayoutManager for this applet. Figure
    9.3 and Figure 9.4 show this applet, with
    the buttons now aligned on the left.

Giving your applet some space

Along with defining the alignment of your user-interface elements, you can also define how much space the applet puts between them. Like alignment, spacing is set once for the applet, and applies to every component. Listing 9.3 and Applet 9.3 demonstrate a right-aligned applet with expanded spacing.

To define spacing with FlowLayout:

1. this.setLayout(new FlowLayout
   → (FlowLayout.RIGHT,35,5));

FlowLayout can be passed either one parameter (as in the previous example) or three. The second parameter is the horizontal spacing between components, and the third parameter is the vertical spacing. In this example, the horizontal spacing is 35 pixels and the vertical spacing is 5 pixels. Figures 9.5 and 9.6 show how these applets look in different browsers.

✔ Tip

■ In this example, we're using the word "component" interchangeably with "user-interface element." In this example, the two are equivalent. Later, we'll see how a component can actually be much more than just a button.

Listing 9.3 Calls Applet 9.3

```
                    Listing
<HTML>
<HEAD>
 <TITLE>Listing 9.3</TITLE>
</HEAD>
<BODY BGCOLOR=WHITE>
 <APPLET CODEBASE="classes" CODE="Applet3.class"
 → WIDTH=400 HEIGHT=150>
 </APPLET>
</BODY>
</HTML>
```

Applet 9.3 This version of the applet displays the buttons right-aligned, with increased horizontal spacing.

```
                    Applet
import java.awt.*;
import java.applet.*;

public class Applet3 extends Applet {

 public void init() {
    String spaces = "        ",buttonText;

    setBackground(Color.white);

    this.setLayout(new FlowLayout
    → (FlowLayout.RIGHT,35,5));
    for (int i=1; i<=10; i++) {
      buttonText = spaces.substring(1,i) +
      → "Button #" + i + spaces.substring(1,i);
      this.add(new Button(buttonText));
    }
 }

}
```

Figure 9.5 These buttons are aligned to the right...

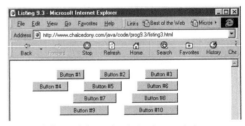

Figure 9.6 ...and show the desired space in between.

Listing 9.4 This HTML file displays the Java Applet in the window.

```
Listing
<HTML>
<HEAD>
 <TITLE>Listing 9.4</TITLE>
</HEAD>
<BODY BGCOLOR=WHITE>
 <APPLET CODEBASE="classes" CODE="Applet4.class"
→ WIDTH=400 HEIGHT=100>
 </APPLET>
</BODY>
</HTML>
```

Applet 9.4 A simple example of a BorderLayout.

```
Applet
import java.awt.*;
import java.applet.*;

public class Applet4 extends Applet {

 public void init() {
   String[] borders =
→{"North","West","Center","East","South"};

   setBackground(Color.white);

   this.setLayout(new BorderLayout(35,5));
   for (int i=0; i<5; i++) {
     this.add(borders[i], new Button(borders[i] +
→ " Button"));
   }
 }

}
```

Figure 9.7 An applet that uses BorderLayout can specify which of five directions each component can be placed.

Figure 9.8 Although only one component can be placed in any given direction.

Using BorderLayout

FlowLayout isn't the only LayoutManager, just the simplest. BorderLayout has a few more capabilities with only a little more complexity. An applet that uses BorderLayout can handle up to five components. Each component is assigned a direction: North, South, East, West, or Center.

The North and South components will be displayed with a width equal to the entire applet area and a height that's just big enough for the button name. The West and East components will take as much height as is necessary to fill up the entire applet area, with a width that's just big enough for the button name. The Center component gets whatever is left over. Listing 9.4 and Applet 9.4 show BorderLayout in use.

To use BorderLayout:

1. this.setLayout(new BorderLayout(35,5));

   This sets the applet's LayoutManager to BorderLayout, with horizontal spacing set to 35 pixels and vertical spacing to 5 pixels.

2. this.add(borders[i], new Button(borders[i] + → " Button"));

   Here we add five buttons, each with a specific border direction (the first para-meter, and a unique name (the second parameter) based on the button's direction. Figures 9.7 and 9.8 show how the applet appears when complete.

Using GridLayout

Another LayoutManager is GridLayout. With GridLayout, an applet can display nicely aligned rows and columns of components. Listing 9.5 and Applet 9.5 demonstrate how to use GridLayout.

To use GridLayout:

1. this.setLayout(new GridLayout(0,3,20,20));

GridLayout can take either two or four parameters. The first two parameters are always the number of rows and the number of columns that the applet should display. If four parameters are present, the third parameter is horizontal spacing and the fourth is vertical spacing. Figure 9.9 and Figure 9.10 show our nice, even grid of buttons.

✔ Tip

■ In this example, the number of rows being passed is zero, and the number of columns is set to three. When one of these two numbers is zero, the true value is calculated based on the other value and the number of components being displayed.

Listing 9.5 This calls Java Applet 9.5.

```
<HTML>
<HEAD>
 <TITLE>Listing 9.5</TITLE>
</HEAD>
<BODY BGCOLOR=WHITE>
 <APPLET CODEBASE="classes" CODE="Applet5.class"
 → WIDTH=400 HEIGHT=100>
 </APPLET>
</BODY>
</HTML>
```

Applet 9.5 A 3 by 3 example of a GridLayout.

```
import java.awt.*;
import java.applet.*;

public class Applet5 extends Applet {

 public void init() {
   setBackground(Color.white);

   this.setLayout(new GridLayout(0,3,20,20));
   for (int i=1; i<10; i++) {
     this.add(new Button(" Button "+i));
   }
 }
}
```

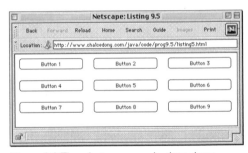

Figure 9.9 Three buttons across by three down...

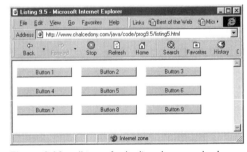

Figure 9.10 ... all in perfectly aligned rows and columns.

Listing 9.6 Displays Applet 9.6.

```
                    Listing
<HTML>
<HEAD>
 <TITLE>Listing 9.6</TITLE>
</HEAD>
<BODY BGCOLOR=WHITE>
 <APPLET CODEBASE="classes" CODE="Applet6.class"
 → WIDTH=400 HEIGHT=100>
 </APPLET>
</BODY>
</HTML>
```

Applet 9.6 Here's how to make your applets stand out.

```
                    Applet
import java.awt.*;
import java.applet.*;

public class Applet6 extends Applet {

 public void init() {
   setBackground(Color.white);

   this.setLayout(new GridLayout(0,3,5,5));
   for (int i=1; i<10; i++) {
     this.add(new Button(" Button "+i));
   }
 }

 public Insets insets() {
   return new Insets(10,10,10,10);
 }

}
```

Standing out with insets

Java allows you to set the margins of a layout by specifying its *inset*. The top, bottom, left, and right-hand margins are all defined, and can help to align your user-interface elements in the window. Listing 9.6 and Applet 9.6 demonstrate usage of the Insets class with a GridLayout.

To set the Insets:

1. public Insets insets() {

   In this statement, we say that the public method insets() will return a value of the class Insets.

2. return new Insets(10,10,10,10);

   In this example, each margin is set to ten pixels. The order of parameters is top, left, bottom, then right. Figure 9.11 and Figure 9.12 display a GridLayout surrounded by a ten-pixel margin.

Figure 9.11 While the Mac and Windows versions do look different...

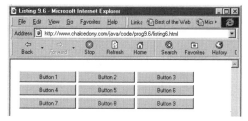

Figure 9.12 ...they both display away from the top left corner.

Using panels to add components

Earlier, we mentioned that components and user-interface elements weren't necessarily the same thing. In this example, we'll see how several user-interface elements can be combined to make a single component using panels.

A container is an abstract Java class that contains components. A window is an example of a container. A *panel* is a special type of container, because it both is contained within a container, and is itself a container. In other words, it can contain components, but it is also itself a component of a window. The elements are added to the panel, and then the panel is added to the window.

Listing 9.7 and Applet 9.7 use a combination of panels and BorderLayout to show how more than five elements can be added to a BorderLayout.

To use a panel:

1. northPanel = new Panel();
   southPanel = new Panel();
   centerPanel = new Panel();
   eastPanel = new Panel();
   westPanel = new Panel();

   Where previously we added five buttons to a GridLayout to fill it up, we're now going to use five panels. Here, we create five new panels, each named with its future direction.

2. for (int i = 1; i<4; i++) {

   The simplest way to add three buttons to each panel is within a loop.

3. northPanel.add(new Button("North #" + i));
   southPanel.add(new Button("South #" + i));
   centerPanel.add(new Button("C #"+i));
   eastPanel.add(new Button("E #" + i));
   westPanel.add(new Button("W #" + i));

Listing 9.7 This HTML file displays Applet 9.7.

```
<HTML>
<HEAD>
 <TITLE>Listing 9.7</TITLE>
</HEAD>
<BODY BGCOLOR=WHITE>
 <APPLET CODEBASE="classes" CODE="Applet7.class"
 ➞ WIDTH=400 HEIGHT=150>
 </APPLET>
</BODY>
</HTML>
```

Applet 9.7 Using a combination of Panels and BorderLayout to get a certain effect.

```
import java.awt.*;
import java.applet.*;

public class Applet7 extends Applet {
  Panel northPanel, southPanel, centerPanel,
  ➞ eastPanel, westPanel;

  public void init() {
    setBackground(Color.white);

    northPanel = new Panel();
    southPanel = new Panel();
    centerPanel = new Panel();
    eastPanel = new Panel();
    westPanel = new Panel();

    for (int i = 1; i<4; i++) {
      northPanel.add(new Button("North #" + i));
      southPanel.add(new Button("South #" + i));
      centerPanel.add(new Button("C #" + i));
      eastPanel.add(new Button("E #" + i));
      westPanel.add(new Button("W #" + i));
    }

    this.setLayout(new BorderLayout(1,1));
    add("North", northPanel);
    add("South", southPanel);
    add("Center", centerPanel);
    add("East", eastPanel);
    add("West", westPanel);
  }
}
```

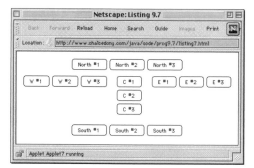

Figure 9.13 This is the effect in a Macintosh

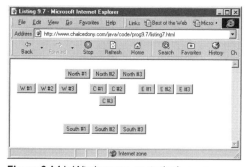

Figure 9.14 In Windows we get similar but not identical results.

In this block, three buttons are added to each panel. Using the loop variable i as part of the button name helps to keep them straight.

4. this.setLayout(new BorderLayout(1,1));

The applet is set to use BorderLayout, with a height and width spacer of one pixel. This does not change the layout of the panels, just the applet. Unless explicitly defined otherwise, the layout for the panels is FlowLayout.

5. add("North", northPanel);
add("South", southPanel);
add("Center", centerPanel);
add("East", eastPanel);
add("West", westPanel);

Here, the panels are added to the applet window, each to its particular direction. Figure 9.13 shows how this appears on a Macintosh. The groups of three buttons appear horizontally in the North, South, East, and West directions. Center gets whatever room is left over, which in this case leaves the three buttons in a column. Figure 9.14 shows the same applet in Windows, where, due to the difference in button size between platforms, two buttons fit in the first Center row.

Using CardLayout

Another Java LayoutManager is CardLayout. CardLayout has one major difference from all the other LayoutManagers: it purposefully doesn't show every element that you put into the window. Instead, each element added to a CardLayout is a new card, which overlays the previously placed element. Think about dealing out a deck of cards one by one, with each card laid carefully over the previous card. Java allows the user to move forward and backward through that deck of cards, always showing just one card at any time.

Listing 9.8 and Applet 9.8 show how to combine Panels with a CardLayout and a BorderLayout to describe the desired page.

To use CardLayout:

1. direction = new Panel();
direction.add(new Button("<"));
direction.add(new Button(">"));

In order to be able to move backwards and forwards through the cards, the user needs some method of navigation. Here, we create a new Panel with two buttons, with a forward and backward arrow. Clicking on each of these buttons will cause the next or previous card to display.

2. cards = new Panel();
layout = new CardLayout();
cards.setLayout(layout);

Here, we first create a new Panel named "cards," and a new CardLayout named "layout." Then, we set the cards Panel to use the layout LayoutManager.

3. for (int i = 0; i<10; i++) {
cards.add(new Button("Card #"+i));
}

This loop adds 10 buttons to the cards Panel, each of which lays on top of the previous button.

Listing 9.8 This displays Applet 9.8 in the browser.

```
Listing
<HTML>
<HEAD>
 <TITLE>Listing 9.8</TITLE>
</HEAD>
<BODY BGCOLOR=WHITE>
 <APPLET CODEBASE="classes" CODE="Applet8.class"
 → WIDTH=400 HEIGHT=100>
 </APPLET>
</BODY>
</HTML>
```

Applet 9.8 CardLayout only shows one card at a time.

```
Applet
import java.awt.*;
import java.applet.*;

public class Applet8 extends Applet {
  Panel cards, direction;
  CardLayout layout;

  public void init() {
    setBackground(Color.white);

    direction = new Panel();
    direction.add(new Button("<"));
    direction.add(new Button(">"));

    cards = new Panel();
    layout = new CardLayout();
    cards.setLayout(layout);
    for (int i = 0; i<10; i++) {
      cards.add(new Button("Card #" + i));
    }

    this.setLayout(new BorderLayout(30,30));
    add("North", direction);
    add("Center", cards);
  }

  public boolean action(Event evt, Object arg) {
    if (evt.target instanceof Component &&
    → ((Component)evt.target).getParent().equals
    →(direction)) {
      if (arg.equals("<")) {
        layout.previous(cards);
        return true;
      }
      if (arg.equals(">")) {
        layout.next(cards);
        return true;
      }
    }
    return super.action(evt, arg);
  }
}
```

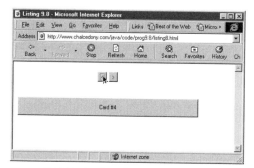

Figure 9.15 Moving from Card #4 to Card #3.

Figure 9.16 Moving from Card #1 to Card #2.

4. this.setLayout(new BorderLayout(30,30));
add("North", direction);
add("Center", cards);

Our overall window is set here to use the BorderLayout LayoutManager, with spacing of 30 pixels in both directions. The "direction" Panel is placed in the North, and the "cards" Panel is placed in the Center.

5. if (arg.equals("<")) {
    layout.previous(cards);
    return true;
}

This code handles the event that occurs when the user clicks on the "<" button. In this case, simply calling the layout.previous() method and passing the "cards" parameter causes, for example, Card #4 to be covered by Card #3, as shown in Figure 9.15.

6. if (arg.equals(">")) {
    layout.next(cards);
    return true;
}

In Figure 9.16, we see a user clicking the ">" button to go from Card#1 to Card #2. This action (clicking the button) triggers an event (this code being called). Here, the layout.next() method with the "cards" parameter, causes the next card in the deck to be displayed.

✔ Tip

■ Note that while we're using BorderLayout, only two of the five directions are in use. While BorderLayout is limited to five maximum directions, there's no limitation on the minimum.

USING CARDLAYOUT

Using GridBagLayout

Yes, that's really what it's called.

GridBagLayout is simulatneously the most complicated and most versatile of all Java's Layout Managers. It supports as many elements as you wish to put in the window, with fairly precise positioning. However, the power does come at a price, that of complexity. Oh, and having to put up with a silly name, too.

Each GridBagLayout consists of one or more GridBagConstraints. Each element's attributes are added to the GridBagConstraint, and then the element itself is added to the GridBagLayout using the variables in GridbagConstraints. Because GridBagConstraints can be used over and over again, any element's variables that are the same as that of the previously added element do not need to be reinitialized.

The simplest way to understand how GridBagLayout works is to envision a grid, with components that are able to cover more than one grid cell. Listing 9.9 and Applet 9.9 show an example of a simple GridBagLayout with 6 buttons in a 5 by 5 grid. Each component specifies how many cells it will take up in each direction, as well as whether or not to expand (and in which directions) if space is available. Figures 9.17 and 9.18 show how this applet appears on different platforms, while Figure 9.19 shows how this layout is based on a 5 by 5 grid.

To use GridBagLayout:

1. GridBagLayout thisLayout =
→ new GridBagLayout();
GridBagConstraints c =
→ new GridBagConstraints();

Here, we create a two new variables: thisLayout, an instance of GridBagLayout, and c, an instance of GridBagConstraints().

2. c.fill = GridBagConstraints.BOTH;

Listing 9.9 This listing displays Applet 9.9 in the browser window.

```
Listing
<HTML>
<HEAD>
  <TITLE>Listing 9.9</TITLE>
</HEAD>
<BODY BGCOLOR=WHITE>
  <APPLET CODEBASE="classes" CODE="Applet9.class"
  → WIDTH=400 HEIGHT=150>
  </APPLET>
</BODY>
</HTML>
```

Figure 9.17 How the applet displays on a Mac.

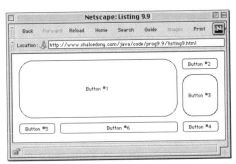

Figure 9.18 And how the applet displays in Windows.

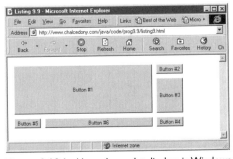

Figure 9.19 This applet is a 5 by 5 grid, with each components taking up a specified amount of space.

Applet 9.9 It's a silly sounding name for a very powerful LayoutManager.

```
================= Applet =================
import java.awt.*;
import java.applet.*;

public class Applet9 extends Applet {
 GridBagLayout thisLayout = new GridBagLayout();
 GridBagConstraints c =
 ⁃ newGridBagConstraints();

 public void init() {
   setBackground(Color.white);
   this.setLayout(thisLayout);

   c.fill = GridBagConstraints.BOTH;
   c.insets = new Insets(5,5,5,5);

   c.gridx = 0;
   c.gridy = 0;
   c.gridwidth = 4;
   c.gridheight = 4;
   c.weightx = 1.0;
   c.weighty = 1.0;
   makeButton(1);

   c.gridx = 4;
   c.gridwidth = 1;
   c.gridheight = 1;
   c.weightx = 0.0;
   c.weighty = 0.0;
   makeButton(2);

   c.gridy = 1;
   c.gridheight = 3;
   makeButton(3);

   c.gridy = 4;
   c.gridheight = 1;
   makeButton(4);

   c.gridx = 0;
   makeButton(5);

   c.gridx = 1;
   c.weightx = 1.0;
   makeButton(6);
 }

 protected void makeButton(int buttonNo) {
   Button newButton = new Button("Button #" +
   ⁃ buttonNo);
   thisLayout.setConstraints(newButton,c);
   add(newButton);
 }
}
```

This line states that all components in this layout should grow in both directions when there is space available. Other valid values for fill can be found in Table 9.1.

3. c.insets = new Insets(5,5,5,5);

Each component in this layout has a margin of 5 pixels on all sides.

4. c.gridx = 0;
c.gridy = 0;

The first component will start with its top left corner in position (0,0).

5. c.gridwidth = 4;
c.gridheight = 4;

This component has a height of 4 grid cells, and a width of 4 grid cells.

6. c.weightx = 1.0;
c.weighty = 1.0;

If there is room in the layout for this component to expand, its growth will have higher priority than any component with a weightx or weighty less than 1, and a lower priority than any component with a weightx or weighty greater than 1.

7. makeButton(1);

This calls a local method with a parameter of 1, which creates a button called "Button #1" with the just-described attributes.

8. c.gridx = 4;
c.gridwidth = 1;
c.gridheight = 1;
c.weightx = 0.0;
c.weighty = 0.0;
makeButton(2);

Here we describe and create a second button. This time the top left corner is at (4,0)—there's no need to specify gridy, because it hasn't changed from the previous button. The width and height of this button is exactly 1 by 1 grid cell, and it has the lowest possible priority for growth in either axis.

9. c.gridy = 1;
c.gridheight = 3;
makeButton(3);

The third button has a top left corner at
(4,1), a width of 1, and a height of 3
grid cells.

10. c.gridy = 4;
c.gridheight = 1;
makeButton(4);

Button 4 has a top left corner of (4,4),
and takes up a 1 by 1 grid cell.

11. c.gridx = 0;
makeButton(5);

Button 5 is identical to button 4, except
that its top left corner is at (0,4).

12. c.gridx = 1;
c.weightx = 1.0;
makeButton(6);

The last button has a top left corner at
(1,4), and would normally have a size
of a 1 by 1 grid cell. However, because
weightx is set to 1, and because no other
components exist, it streches along the
x-axis to fill the available area.

13. protected void makeButton(int buttonNo) {
   Button newButton = newButton("Button
   → #" + buttonNo);
   thisLayout.setConstraints(newButton,c);
   add(newButton);
}

The makeButton() method creates a
button, with a label that is built using
the numeric parameter passed to it.
The setConstraints() method takes a component and a GridBagConstraints object,
and associates the GridBagConstraints
object with that component. The new
button, now associated with the specified
GridBagConstraints, is then added to
the layout.

Table 9.1

GridBagConstraints variables

NAME	VALID CONSTANTS (DEFAULT IN ITALICS)	DESCRIPTION
anchor	CENTER, EAST, NORTH, NORTHEAST, NORTHWEST, SOUTH, SOUTHEAST, SOUTHWEST, WEST	Specifies where to display the component when the available cell area is larger than the component
fill	BOTH, HORIZONTAL, NONE, VERTICAL	Specifies in which direction a component should grow if there is room available
gridheight	REMAINDER	The height of the component, measured in grid cells; default is 1
gridwidth	REMAINDER	The width of the component, measured in grid cells; default is 1
gridx	RELATIVE	The x-axis position of the component, as seen on a grid
gridy	RELATIVE	The y-axis position of the component, as seen on a grid
insets	–	Specfies the margins for a component; default is (0,0,0,0)
ipadx	–	Specifies the amount of internal padding added to a component in the x-axis; default is 0
ipady	–	Specifies the amount of internal padding added to a component in the y-axis; default is 0
weightx	–	Specifies how this component should expand in the x-axis compared to other components; the higher the number, the higher the priority; default is 0.0
weighty	–	Specifies how this component should expand in the y-axis compared to other components; the higher the number, the higher the priority; default is 0.0

USING GRIDBAGLAYOUT

MAKING YOUR PAGES MOVE

One area where Java shines in comparison to HTML or JavaScript is in its handling of images and animation. You can use Java to display a simple image, or just a part of an image. Java can display a single image in a random location, or a random image in a single location.

Animated GIFs are common on the Web to handle simple animation. But with Java, you can have animation that responds to the user, or animation that follows a random instead of a set sequence.

There are some pretty tricky concepts here, so follow along closely, keep your hands inside while the pages are moving, and please—no flash photography.

Displaying an image

In the same way a journey starts with but a single step, displaying moving pictures starts with just a single image. Applet 10.1 puts an image into your Java window.

This example assumes that you have 52 images corresponding to a normal deck of playing cards. The cards are named card1.gif to card52.gif, and the goal is to display one in the browser window.

To display an image:

1. int randomCard;

   First we create a new integer object named randomCard.

2. setBackground(Color.black);
   randomCard = (int)(java.lang.Math.random()
   → * 52)+1;

   Here the background is set to black. The HTML, as shown in Listing 10.1, gives the applet a very small area, so the black background puts a small frame around the displayed card. We then initialize randomCard to be a random number between 1 and 52, signifying which playing card to display.

3. thisCard = getImage(getCodeBase(), "card"
   → +randomCard+".gif");

   Here's where we load the card. The getImage() method has two parameters: the directory that contains the image, and the name of the image. The getCodeBase() method says that the image is in the same directory as the .class file, and the image name is calculated and assembled based on the random number generated in step 3.

Listing 10.1 Display the applet in the browser window

```
Listing
<HTML>
<HEAD>
 <TITLE>Listing 10.1</TITLE>
</HEAD>
<BODY BGCOLOR=WHITE>
 <APPLET CODEBASE="classes" CODE="Applet1.class"
 → WIDTH=47 HEIGHT=65>
 </APPLET>
</BODY>
</HTML>
```

Applet 10.1 This applet displays a random image on a page

```
Applet
import java.awt.*;
import java.applet.*;

public class Applet1 extends Applet {
  Image thisCard;

  public void init() {
    int randomCard;

    setBackground(Color.black);
    randomCard = (int)(java.lang.Math.random() *
    → 52)+1;
    thisCard = getImage(getCodeBase(),"card"+
    →randomCard+".gif");
  }

  public void paint(Graphics g) {
    g.drawImage(thisCard,2,2,this);
  }

}
```

Figure 10.1 This is one card displayed

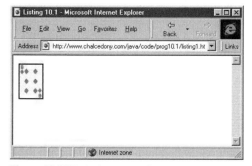

Figure 10.2 This is the next card

4. public void paint(Graphics g) {
        g.drawImage(thisCard,2,2,this);
    }

The paint() method is where we call draw-Image() to display the card in the browser, as shown in Figures 10.1 and 10.2.

Displaying part of an image

Dealing with 52 separate images can be a pain. In this example, all 52 images have been combined into one big image (Figure 10.3) and Java will pick out just the one card we want to display. Listing 10.2 and Applet 10.2 show how to display just part of an image.

To display part of an image:

1. ImageFilter cardFilter;
   ImageProducer cardProducer;

   Here are two new classes we've never seen before. In order to select part of an image, Java needs to know two things: the dimensions of the desired area, and what image we want to act upon. These are the variables that will handle the selection area.

2. playingCards = getImage(getCodeBase(),
   → "cards.gif");

   Here we read in the big image.

3. cardHeight = 61;
   cardWidth = 43;

   To get just the image we want, we'll need the height and width of a single card.

4. cardPos = (randomCard*cardWidth)+1;

   The starting position of the desired image is calculated by multiplying the number of the card (starting from 0) we want by the width of the cards and adding 1. For example, if we want the first card, cardPos is (0 x 43) + 1, or 1. For the fifth card, cardPos is (4 x 43) + 1, or 173. This number tells us how many pixels from the right our desired card starts.

5. cardFilter = new CropImageFilter(cardPos, 1,
   → cardWidth, cardHeight);

   The cardFilter variable is set up with the desired window into the big image. That is, cardFilter now contains the coordinates of the image we actually want so that we

Listing 10.2 This HTML calls the applet

```
<HTML>
<HEAD>
 <TITLE>Listing 10.2</TITLE>
</HEAD>
<BODY BGCOLOR=WHITE>
 <APPLET CODEBASE="classes" CODE="Applet2.class"
 → WIDTH=47 HEIGHT=65>
 </APPLET>
</BODY>
</HTML>
```

Applet 10.2 Applet to display part of an image

```
import java.awt.*;
import java.applet.*;
import java.awt.image.*;

public class Applet2 extends Applet {
  Image thisCard;

  public void init() {
    int randomCard,cardPos,cardWidth,cardHeight;
    Image playingCards;
    ImageFilter cardFilter;
    ImageProducer cardProducer;

    setBackground(Color.black);

    playingCards = getImage(getCodeBase(),
    → "cards.gif");
    randomCard = (int)(java.lang.Math.random() *
    →52);
    cardHeight =  61;
    cardWidth =  43;
    cardPos = (randomCard*cardWidth)+1;
    cardFilter = new CropImageFilter(cardPos,1,
    → cardWidth,cardHeight);
    cardProducer = new FilteredImageSource
    → (playingCards.getSource(),cardFilter);
    thisCard = createImage(cardProducer);
  }

  public void paint(Graphics g) {
    g.drawImage(thisCard,2,2,this);
  }

}
```

Figure 10.3 The entire deck of cards in one file

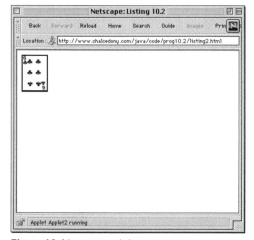

Figure 10.4 Just one card shown

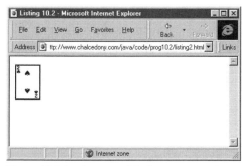

Figure 10.5 Another part of the larger image is shown

can grab just that area from within the full-size image.

6. cardProducer = new FilteredImageSource
→ (playingCards.getSource(),cardFilter);

The cardProducer variable uses the Filtered-ImageSource() method with the source of the large image and the filter area from the last step.

7. thisCard = createImage(cardProducer);

The cardProducer from step 6 is passed to the createImage() method to create a new, small image of a single playing card, as shown in Figures 10.4 and 10.5.

DISPLAYING PART OF AN IMAGE

Drawing a border around an image

In the previous two tasks, we made the image appear to have a border around it by simply making the applet area slightly larger than the image we were displaying. Obviously, this technique won't always work. In this example, as shown in Listing 10.3 and Applet 10.3, we manually draw a border around our image, for a more versatile (and visually pleasing) effect.

To draw a border around an image:

1. g.drawRoundRect(1,1,cardWidth+2,
   → cardHeight+2,5,5);

   The drawRoundRect() method takes six parameters: the x and y of the starting point, the width of the frame, the height of the frame, and the width and height of the angle of the corners (i.e., distance from the edge). Figures 10.6 and 10.7 display the single-pixel line around the image.

Listing 10.3 Set up your HTML

```
<HTML>
<HEAD>
 <TITLE>Listing 10.3</TITLE>
</HEAD>
<BODY BGCOLOR=WHITE>
 <APPLET CODEBASE="classes" CODE="Applet3.class"
 →WIDTH=300 HEIGHT=100>
 </APPLET>
</BODY>
</HTML>
```

Applet 10.3 The border applet

```
import java.awt.*;
import java.applet.*;
import java.awt.image.*;

public class Applet3 extends Applet {
  Image thisCard;
  int cardWidth=43,cardHeight=61;

  public void init() {
    int randomCard,cardPos;
    Image playingCards;
    ImageFilter cardFilter;
    ImageProducer cardProducer;

    setBackground(Color.white);

    playingCards = getImage(getCodeBase(),
    →"cards.gif");
    randomCard = (int)(java.lang.Math.random() *
    →52);
    cardPos = (randomCard*cardWidth)+1;
    cardFilter = new CropImageFilter(cardPos,1,
    →cardWidth,cardHeight);
    cardProducer = new FilteredImageSource
    →(playingCards.getSource(),cardFilter);
    thisCard = createImage(cardProducer);
  }

  public void paint(Graphics g) {
    g.drawImage(thisCard,3,3,this);
    g.drawRoundRect(1,1,cardWidth+2,cardHeight+2,
    →5,5);
  }

}
```

Figure 10.6 Shows a border of 1 pixel

Figure 10.7 This card also shows a border

✔ Tips

■ If we wanted sharp corners instead of curved corners, this applet could use the drawRect() method instead of drawRound → Rect(). The parameters of drawRect() are just the first four parameters of drawRound → Rect().

■ The appearance of the frame can vary dramatically depending on the values passed for the height and width of the angle of the corners. The larger the numbers, the more rounded the frame. If the numbers are large enough, you'll end up with a circle instead of a rectangle.

Displaying multiple images

In this example, Listing 10.4 and Applet 10.4 display five random images instead of one.

To display multiple images:

1. Image thisCard[] = new Image[imgCt];

Instead of creating thisCard as an Image object, we make thisCard an array of Image objects.

2. boolean usedCards[] = new boolean[52];

The usedCards array of Booleans (true/false values) stores whether a given card has already been displayed. All the values are initialized as false.

3. for (i=0;i<imgCt;i++) {
    randomCard = (int)(java.lang.Math.random
    → () * 52);
    if (usedCards[randomCard]) {
        i—;
    }

For each card that we want to display, we go through this loop. A random card is picked, and then usedCards is checked to see if that one has already been used. If so, we subtract one from i so that this pass through the loop doesn't count.

4. thisCard[i] = createImage(cardProducer);
usedCards[randomCard] = true;

If this card hasn't been seen already, its image is put into the thisCard array and its usage in usedCards is set to true.

5. startPt = (i*(cardWidth+10));
g.drawImage(thisCard[i],startPt+3,3,this);
g.drawRoundRect(startPt+1,1,cardWidth+2,
→ cardHeight+2,5,5);

Because there are five images, there's no fixed starting point at which to display each image. The startPt variable calculates where each should start, based on which

Listing 10.4 HTML! HTML! We love HTML!

```
<HTML>
<HEAD>
  <TITLE>Listing 10.4</TITLE>
</HEAD>
<BODY BGCOLOR=WHITE>
  <APPLET CODEBASE="classes" CODE="Applet4.class"
  →WIDTH=600 HEIGHT=100>
  </APPLET>
</BODY>
</HTML>
```

Applet 10.4 This applet displays 5 random images

```
import java.awt.*;
import java.applet.*;
import java.awt.image.*;

public class Applet4 extends Applet {
  int cardWidth=43,cardHeight=61,imgCt=5;
  Image thisCard[] = new Image[imgCt];

  public void init() {
    int randomCard,cardPos,i;
    Image playingCards;
    ImageFilter cardFilter;
    ImageProducer cardProducer;
    boolean usedCards[] = new boolean[52];

    setBackground(Color.white);
    playingCards = getImage(getCodeBase(),
    →"cards.gif");

    for (i=0;i<imgCt;i++) {
      randomCard = (int)(java.lang.Math.random() *
      →52);
      if (usedCards[randomCard]) {
        i—;
      }
      else {
        cardPos = (randomCard*cardWidth)+1;
        cardFilter = new CropImageFilter
        →(cardPos,1,cardWidth,cardHeight);
        cardProducer = new FilteredImageSource
        →(playingCards.getSource(),cardFilter);
        thisCard[i] = createImage(cardProducer);
        usedCards[randomCard] = true;
      }
    }
  }

  public void paint(Graphics g) {
    int i,startPt;

    for (i=0;i<imgCt;i++) {
      startPt = (i*(cardWidth+10));
      g.drawImage(thisCard[i],startPt+3,3,this);
      g.drawRoundRect(startPt+1,1,cardWidth+2,
      →cardHeight+2,5,5);
    }
  }
}
```

Figure 10.8 Pick a card, any card.

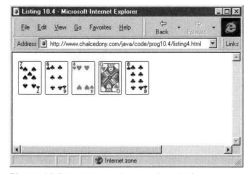

Figure 10.9 Another card on another platform.

pass through the loop we're on and the width of the cards.

The drawImage() and drawRoundRect() methods are similar to what we've seen before, except that the former now uses the thisCard array for the card to display, and both use startPt to know where to start drawing, as shown in Figures 10.8 and 10.9.

✔ Tip

■ Note how easy it is to change the number of images that are displayed: Simply change imgCt=5 to some other number, and everything else changes with it.

Threading and animation

You may have noticed that all the examples you've seen so far in this chapter involve just putting something up on the screen. They don't move and they don't change. The key to making Java applets move and change is *threading*, as demonstrated here.

When a computer does more than one thing at a time, it is referred to as *multi-threaded*. Each of the things it is doing is called a *thread*. Threads let programs play nice with other programs, and with other parts of the same program. Java (and your operating system) parcel out time to threads, making sure that each gets the time it needs without hogging your computer.

To make an applet threaded:

1. public class Applet5 extends Applet
→ implements Runnable {

The big change here is that we're not just extending Applet anymore, we're also *implementing* Runnable. This adds the run() method to the applet, which means that Java will now be able to do things while the applet is running. Previously, we've only been able to change the screen display when it was first displayed, or when the user caused an event to occur. Now, Java will be able to use run() to do just about anything.

2. Thread runner;

This creates a new type of object, a thread called runner, which will handle the one thread that this applet needs.

3. public void start() {
    runner = new Thread(this);
    runner.start();
}

Because we're using threading, we now need to override the start() method. We create our new thread and tell it to start up.

Listing 10.5 The HTML you need to load the applet

```
<HTML>
<HEAD>
 <TITLE>Listing 10.5</TITLE>
</HEAD>
<BODY BGCOLOR=WHITE>
 <APPLET CODEBASE="classes" CODE="Applet5.class"
 ↪WIDTH=300 HEIGHT=100>
 </APPLET>
</BODY>
</HTML>
```

Applet 10.5 The applet itself.

```
                  Applet
import java.awt.*;
import java.applet.*;
import java.awt.image.*;

public class Applet5 extends Applet implements
→Runnable {
 int cardWidth=43,cardHeight=61,imgCt=10,
 →thisPos;
 Image currImg,thisCard[] = new Image[imgCt];
 Thread runner;

 public void init() {
   int randomCard,cardPos,i;
   Image playingCards;
   ImageFilter cardFilter;
   ImageProducer cardProducer;
   boolean usedCards[] = new boolean [52];

   setBackground(Color.white);
   playingCards = getImage
   → (getCodeBase(),"cards.gif");

   for (i=0;i<imgCt;i++) {
     randomCard = (int)(java.lang.Math.random() *
     →52);
     if (usedCards[randomCard]) {
       i--;
     }
     else {
       cardPos = (randomCard*cardWidth)+1;
       cardFilter = newCropImageFilter
       →(cardPos,1,cardWidth,cardHeight);
       cardProducer = new FilteredImageSource
       →(playingCards.getSource(),cardFilter);
       thisCard[i] = createImage(cardProducer);
       usedCards[randomCard] = true;
     }
   }
   thisPos = (int)(java.lang.Math.random() *
   →200);
   currImg = thisCard[0];
 }

 public void start() {
   runner = new Thread(this);
   runner.start();
 }

 public void run() {
   for (int i=1;i<imgCt;i++) {
     try {
       Thread.sleep(2000);
     }
     catch (InterruptedException e) {
     }

     thisPos = (int)(java.lang.Math.random() *
     →200);
     currImg = thisCard[i];
     repaint();
   }
 }

 public void paint(Graphics g) {
   g.drawImage(currImg,thisPos+3,3,this);
   g.drawRoundRect(thisPos+1,1,cardWidth+2,
   →cardHeight+2,5,5);
 }
}
```

4. public void run() {

Here's where the action is. The run() method is called whenever your computer gives Java a chance to do something.

5. for (int i=1;i<imgCt;i++) {

What we want to do is display our ten images, so we loop through them.

6. try {
　　　Thread.sleep(2000);
　　}

Whenever you have a run() method, you have to have a try/catch statement. Other threads are giving up system time to your applet, so your applet should be a good neighbor and give control back to the system periodically.

Here we tell the thread to sleep for two seconds (2000 milliseconds). If something bad happens while the applet is sleeping, the try will throw the error to the catch statement.

7. catch (InterruptedException e) {
　　}

If, during our two-second sleep, something interrupts the thread, a Interrupted → Exception will be thrown, and so must be caught. Here we catch it, but because we don't care about interruptions, we don't have to do anything else with it.

8. thisPos = (int)(java.lang.Math.random() *
　　→ 200);
currImg = thisCard[i];
repaint();

The variable thisPos picks a random location at which to display currImg, our random card. We then call the repaint() method, which will clear the applet area and then call paint(). Because repaint() clears the applet area (by calling update()), only one card at a time is displayed, as shown in Figures 10.10 and 10.11.

✔ Tip

- You might wonder sometimes how to know what errors your applet needs to catch. Here's an easy way to figure out the most important ones: don't catch any errors. If some are required, your compiler will object and tell you what exceptions need to be caught before it will create your .class file.

Figure 10.10 The cards appear ...

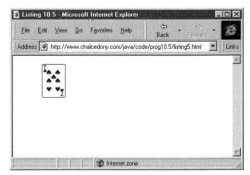

Figure 10.11 ... to move and change.

Listing 10.6 The HTML

```
Listing
<HTML>
<HEAD>
 <TITLE>Listing 10.6</TITLE>
</HEAD>
<BODY BGCOLOR=WHITE>
 <APPLET CODEBASE="classes" CODE="Applet6.class"
 →WIDTH=300 HEIGHT=100>
 </APPLET>
</BODY>
</HTML>
```

Applet 10.6 This applet gets rid of the flicker

```
Applet
import java.awt.*;
import java.applet.*;
import java.awt.image.*;

public class Applet6 extends Applet implements
→Runnable {
 int cardWidth=43,cardHeight=61,imgCt=50,
 →thisPos;
 Image currImg,thisCard[] = new Image[imgCt],
 →winScratch;
 Graphics gScratch;
 Thread runner;

 public void init() {
   int randomCard,cardPos,i;
   Image playingCards;
   ImageFilter cardFilter;
   ImageProducer cardProducer;
   boolean usedCards[] = new boolean [52];

   winScratch = createImage(this.size().width,
   →this.size().height);
   gScratch = winScratch.getGraphics();
   setBackground(Color.white);
   playingCards = getImage(getCodeBase(),
   →"cards.gif");

   for (i=0;i<imgCt;i++) {
     randomCard = (int)(java.lang.Math.random() *
     →52);
     if (usedCards[randomCard]) {
       i--;
     }
     else {
       cardPos = (randomCard*cardWidth)+1;
       cardFilter = new
       CropImageFilter(cardPos,1,
       →cardWidth,cardHeight);
       cardProducer = new FilteredImageSource
       →(playingCards.getSource(),cardFilter);
       thisCard[i] = createImage(cardProducer);
       usedCards[randomCard] = true;
     }
   }
   thisPos = (int)(java.lang.Math.random() *
   →200);
   currImg = thisCard[0];
 }
```

Continued on next page

Double-buffering animation

You may have noticed that the images in the last example flickered when they were drawn on your screen. Listing 10.6 and Applet 10.6 show you how to use a technique called *double-buffering* to get rid of that flicker.

As mentioned in the previous task, the applet area is completely redrawn each time a new card is displayed, causing the flickering. The double-buffering solution creates an off-screen (or "scratch") drawing area, updating that instead of the on-screen area, and then using the off-screen area to update the screen after everything has been drawn. This means that the on-screen area the user sees is updated once, not twice, eliminating the flicker.

To double-buffer animation:

1. Image   currImg,thisCard[] = new Image
   → [imgCt],winScratch;
   Graphics   gScratch;

   Here's where we create the off-screen scratch area in memory, with an Image object named winScratch and a Graphics object named gScratch.

2. winScratch = createImage(this.size().width,
   → this.size().height);
   gScratch = winScratch.getGraphics();

   We initialize winScratch, our scratch area, to be an image with the exact dimensions of the applet area. gScratch is initialized using winScratch's getGraphics() method.

3. gScratch.setColor(this.getBackground());
   gScratch.fillRect(0,0,this.size().width,
   → this.size().height);
   gScratch.setColor(Color.black);
   gScratch.drawImage(currImg, thisPos+3,3,
   → this);
   gScratch.drawRoundRect(thisPos+1,1,
   → cardWidth+2,cardHeight+2,5,5);
   g.drawImage(winScratch,0,0,this);

Because we now have to handle all the screen updates manually, a few lines have been added to the paint() method. The big change is that instead of calling g.drawImage() (for instance), we're calling gScratch.drawImage(). This is where the double-buffering, i.e., the writing out to the off-screen buffer, is occurring. Only in the last line, when the off-screen area has been completely drawn, is g.drawImage() called, with a parameter of winScratch. This puts the off-screen image into the on-screen area, as demonstrated by Figures 10.12 and 10.13.

4. public final void update(Graphics g) {
    paint(g);
}

A required part of double-buffering is overriding the update() method. It's the update() method that clears the screen normally, so in order to stop that behavior, the method must be overridden. We still want drawing to take place, however, so we still call the paint() method.

Applet 10.6 *continued*

```
public void start() {
  runner = new Thread(this);
  runner.start();
}

public void run() {
  for (int i=1;i<imgCt;i++) {
    try {
      Thread.sleep(2000);
    }
    catch (InterruptedException e) {
    }

    thisPos = (int)(java.lang.Math.random() *
    →200);
    currImg = thisCard[i];
    repaint();
  }
}

public void paint(Graphics g) {
  gScratch.setColor(this.getBackground());
  gScratch.fillRect
  →(0,0,this.size().width,this.size().height);
  gScratch.setColor(Color.black);

  gScratch.drawImage(currImg,thisPos+3,3,this);
  gScratch.drawRoundRect
  →(thisPos+1,1,cardWidth+2,cardHeight+2,5,5);
  g.drawImage(winScratch,0,0,this);
}

public final void update(Graphics g) {
  paint(g);
}
}
```

Figure 10.12 No flicker as this card...

Figure 10.13 ...changes to this card.

Listing 10.7 Calls Applet 10.7

```
<HTML>
<HEAD>
  <TITLE>Listing 10.7</TITLE>
</HEAD>
<BODY BGCOLOR=WHITE>
  <APPLET CODEBASE="classes" CODE="Applet7.class"
  →WIDTH=300 HEIGHT=100>
  </APPLET>
</BODY>
</HTML>
```

Figure 10.14 There's no end...

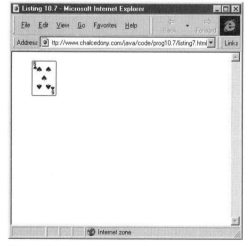

Figure 10.15 ... to this house of cards.

Displaying unlimited images

Sometimes it's useful to only display a certain number of images. Other times, you'll want to continue an animation indefinitely. This example displays a random playing card every 2 seconds for as long as you're on the Web page.

To display non-stop animation:

1. while (true) {

   Instead of looping a certain number of times inside run(), this statement (which always evaluates to true) forces the animation to continue forever.

2. if (currImg != null) {

   Because all the image initialization code has been moved to the run() method, there's a short amount of time when paint() has been called but currImg has not yet been set. Checking to see if currImg has been set before attempting to draw it on the screen avoids errors. Figures 10.14 and 10.15 show how this applet appears on screen.

   For the most part, this example is very similar to the previous. Most of the changes just involve code that's been moved, not added, as seen in Listing 10.7 and Applet 10.7.

Applet 10.7 This applet is similar to Applet 10.6

```
                                Applet

import java.awt.*;
import java.applet.*;
import java.awt.image.*;

public class Applet7 extends Applet implements Runnable {
 int cardWidth=43,cardHeight=61,thisPos;
 Image winScratch,playingCards,currImg;
 Graphics gScratch;
 Thread runner;

 public void init() {
    winScratch = createImage(this.size().width,this.size().height);
    gScratch = winScratch.getGraphics();
    setBackground(Color.white);
    playingCards = getImage(getCodeBase(),"cards.gif");
 }

 public void start() {
    runner = new Thread(this);
    runner.start();
 }

 public void run() {
    int randomCard,cardPos;
    ImageFilter cardFilter;
    ImageProducer cardProducer;

    while (true) {
      try {
        Thread.sleep(2000);
      }
      catch (InterruptedException e) {
      }

      thisPos = (int)(java.lang.Math.random() * 200);
      randomCard = (int)(java.lang.Math.random() * 52);
      cardPos = (randomCard*cardWidth)+1;
      cardFilter = new CropImageFilter(cardPos,1,cardWidth,cardHeight);
      cardProducer = new FilteredImageSource(playingCards.getSource(),cardFilter);
      currImg = createImage(cardProducer);
      repaint();
    }
 }

 public void paint(Graphics g) {
    if (currImg != null) {
      gScratch.setColor(this.getBackground());
      gScratch.fillRect(0,0,this.size().width,this.size→().height);
      gScratch.setColor(Color.black);

      gScratch.drawImage(currImg,thisPos+3,3,this);
      gScratch.drawRoundRect(thisPos+1,1,cardWidth+2,cardHeight+2,5,5);
      g.drawImage(winScratch,0,0,this);
    }
 }

 public final void update(Graphics g) {
    paint(g);
 }
}
```

Listing 10.8 This HTML loads Applet 10.8

```
                          Listing
<HTML>
<HEAD>
 <TITLE>Listing 10.8</TITLE>
</HEAD>
<BODY BGCOLOR=WHITE>
 <APPLET CODEBASE="classes" CODE="Applet8.class"
→WIDTH=300 HEIGHT=100>
 </APPLET>
</BODY>
</HTML>
```

Applet 10.8 This applet lets your visitors stop and start the animations

```
                          Applet
import java.awt.*;
import java.applet.*;
import java.awt.image.*;

public class Applet8 extends Applet implements
→Runnable {
 int cardWidth=43,cardHeight=61,thisPos;
 Image winScratch,playingCards,currImg;
 Graphics gScratch;
 Thread runner;
 Button startStop;
 boolean isRunning = true;

 public void init() {
   winScratch = createImage
   →(this.size().width,this.size().height);
   gScratch = winScratch.getGraphics();
   setBackground(Color.white);
   playingCards = getImage(getCodeBase(),
   →"cards.gif");
   startStop = new Button("Stop");
   add(startStop);
 }

 public void start() {
   if (runner == null) {
     runner = new Thread(this);
     runner.start();
   }
 }

 public void stop() {
   runner = null;
 }

 public void run() {
   int randomCard,cardPos;
   ImageFilter cardFilter;
   ImageProducer cardProducer;
```

Continued on next page

Controlling animation

Letting your animation run on and on (and on and on...) is nice, but it's nicer to be able to start and stop the display. Listing 10.8 and Applet 10.8 include a button that allows the user to stop the display and then start it back up again.

To start and stop animation:

1. Button startStop;
   boolean isRunning = true;

   Two variables are declared here: startStop, a button which does exactly what it says, and isRunning, which keeps track of whether or not the applet is running. It's set to start off running.

2. startStop = new Button("Stop");
   add(startStop);

   The new button is added to the display with a label of "Stop."

3. if (runner == null) {

   Previously, we made the assumption that if start() was called, it was time to start up a new thread. Now, because the thread can be started and stopped, we have to check to see if it already exists before trying to create it.

4. public void stop() {
        runner = null;
   }

   Here's a new method: stop(). Now that the thread can be stopped as well as started, we need to handle that option. In this case, all we're going to do is throw away our runner thread.

5. while (isRunning) {

   In the last example, we looped through run() forever. Now, we just want to do it while the isRunning flag is true.

6. if (currImg != null && isRunning) {

Along with not wanting to paint nonexistent images, we now also want to skip painting whenever the isRunning flag has been set to false. The results on the screen are displayed in Figures 10.16 and 10.17.

7. if (isRunning) {
        isRunning = false;
        startStop.setLabel("Start");
        stop();
    }

When the Start/Stop button is pressed, we check to see if we're currently running or not. If we are, we want to stop the thread. In this case, the isRunning flag is turned off (false), the button label is reset to "Start," and stop() is called.

8. else {
        isRunning = true;
        startStop.setLabel("Stop");
        start();
    }

If we were stopped, it's time to start back up again. We set the isRunning flag to on (true), reset the button label back to "Stop," and call the start() method to restart the thread.

Applet 10.8 *continued*

```
    while (isRunning) {
      try {
        Thread.sleep(2000);
      }
      catch (InterruptedException e) {
      }

      thisPos = (int)(java.lang.Math.random() *
      →200);
      randomCard = (int)(java.lang.Math.random() *
      →52);
      cardPos = (randomCard*cardWidth)+1;
      cardFilter = new CropImageFilter
      →(cardPos,1,cardWidth,cardHeight);
      cardProducer = new FilteredImageSource
      →(playingCards.getSource(),cardFilter);
      currImg = createImage(cardProducer);
      repaint();
    }
  }

public void paint(Graphics g) {
    if (currImg != null && isRunning) {
      gScratch.setColor(this.getBackground());
      gScratch.fillRect(0,0,this.size()
      →.width,this.size().height);
      gScratch.setColor(Color.black);

      gScratch.drawImage(currImg,thisPos+3,
      →32,this);
      gScratch.drawRoundRect(thisPos+1,
      →30,cardWidth+2,cardHeight+2,5,5);
      g.drawImage(winScratch,0,0,this);
    }
  }

public final void update(Graphics g) {
    paint(g);
  }

public boolean action(Event e, Object arg) {
    if (e.target instanceof Button) {
      if (isRunning) {
        isRunning = false;
        startStop.setLabel("Start");
        stop();
      }
      else {
        isRunning = true;
        startStop.setLabel("Stop");
        start();
      }
      return true;
    }
    return false;
  }
}
```

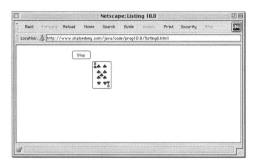

Figure 10.16 How the button looks in Netscape Navigator on the Mac

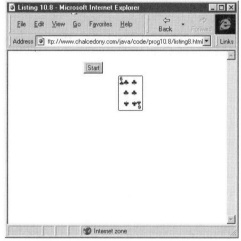

Figure 10.17 The same button in Internet Explorer on Microsoft Windows.

✔ Tip

- You can add another form field (a radio button, text box, etc.) to allow the user to modify how long the applet sleeps between redraws.

CONTROLLING ANIMATION

JAVA AND JAVASCRIPT

At first glance, Java and JavaScript might appear to be related, given the similarities in their names. The truth is that they have many more differences than similarities.

When Sun first introduced Java to the world in 1995 it was widely acknowledged as a major change in programming languages. Around the same time, Netscape introduced a scripting language called LiveScript, which was an addon to HTML for Netscape. A few months later, those smart guys (and gals) at Netscape noticed that no one was paying attention to their new language due to the amount of buzz Java was getting, so they decided to borrow a little of that buzz for themselves by changing the name of their language to JavaScript. Mostly, they succeeded in badly confusing legions of would-be Web programmers.

However, JavaScript and Java can and do talk to each other, giving additional functionality to your pages. With this approach, you can use each language for its strengths, combining the two for a sum greater than the parts.

If you're interested in learning more about JavaScript, a good place to start is *JavaScript for the World Wide Web, Visual QuickStart Guide, 2nd Edition*, (Peachpit Press; 1998) written by Tom Negrino and myself.

Checking for Java

You can use JavaScript in your HTML page to check to see if Java is enabled. Doing this allows you to generate different pages on the fly, depending on whether or not the user has Java.

To check if Java is enabled:

1. <SCRIPT LANGUAGE="JAVASCRIPT">

   The SCRIPT HTML tag tells the browser that whatever follows is scripting language, not text to be displayed in the browser window. The LANGUAGE attribute of the SCRIPT tag tells the browser which scripting language we're using, which in this case is JavaScript.

2. <!— Hide script from old browsers

   The first line of a script should always start with a comment. This is so older browsers that don't understand JavaScript will skip the contents of the script, thinking that the entire script is a comment.

3. if (navigator.javaEnabled()) {

   Here's the meat of the script. JavaScript has an object called navigator, which has a method called javaEnabled(). This method is either true or false, depending on whether this browser understands Java. If the check evaluates to true, the code within the following curly braces will be executed.

4. document.writeln('<APPLET CODEBASE= → "classes" CODE="Applet5.class" WIDTH= → 400 → HEIGHT=300></APPLET>')

   If JavaScript is enabled, the method document.writeln() will be executed. This method adds whatever's been passed to the page's HTML. In this case, we're adding an APPLET tag. Figure 11.1 and Figure 11.2 show the results of Listing 11.1 in Java-enabled browsers.

Listing 11.1 Displays an applet if Java's enabled

```
<HTML>
<HEAD>
 <TITLE>Listing 11.1</TITLE>
</HEAD>
<BODY BGCOLOR=WHITE>

 <SCRIPT LANGUAGE="JAVASCRIPT">
   <!-- Hide script from old browsers

   if (navigator.javaEnabled()) {
     document.writeln('<APPLET CODEBASE="classes"
     → CODE="Applet5.class" WIDTH=400
     → HEIGHT=300></APPLET>')
   }
   else {
     document.writeln('<A HREF=
     → "http://www.netscape.com/comprod/mirror/
     → index.html"><IMG SRC=
     → "http://www.netscape.com/comprod/mirror/
     → images/netscape_now_anim.gif"
     → WIDTH=90 HEIGHT=30 BORDER=0></A><BR>
     → Download a java-enabled browser now!')
   }

   // End hiding script from old browsers -->
 </SCRIPT>

</BODY>
</HTML>
```

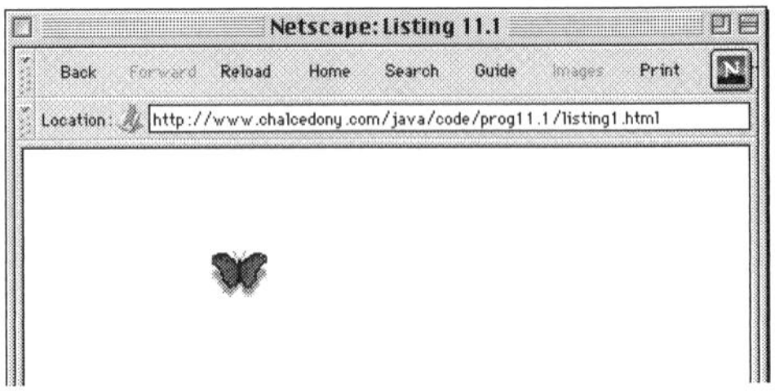

Figure 11.1 How the applet looks in a Java-enabled browser

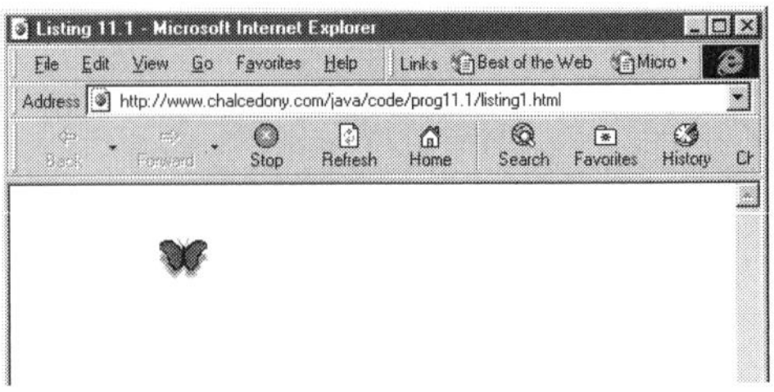

Figure 11.2 The same page in Internet Explorer

Figure 11.3 This is displayed if the user has JavaScript turned on but not Java.

5.   }

This right curly brace ends the **true** code segment.

6.   else {

If the above check to see if Java is enabled fails (i.e., Java is not enabled), the code in the **else** code block is executed.

7.   document.writeln('<A HREF="http://www.
   → netscape.com/comprod/mirror/index.
   → html"><IMG SRC="http://www.
   → netscape.com/comprod/mirror/images/
   → netscape_now_anim.gif" WIDTH=90
   → HEIGHT=30 BORDER=0></A>
   → Download a java-enabled browser
   → now!')

This code encourages the user to get a current version of a Java-enabled browser, as shown in Figure 11.3.

8.   }

This right curly brace ends the **false** or **else** code segment.

9.   // End hiding script from old browsers —>

For those older browsers that don't understand SCRIPT tags, this ends the comment started above.

10.   </SCRIPT>

This ends the JavaScript part of the page.

✔ Tips

■ The **else** part of the script is optional. If there's something that you want to add only if Java's enabled, leave off the **else** block.

■ Most modern browsers allow the user to turn both JavaScript and Java on or off. The code above will work only if JavaScript is turned on but Java is turned off.

JavaScript and public Java methods

If a user is running a Netscape browser with both JavaScript and Java enabled, JavaScript is able to access public Java methods. This is accomplished via a Netscape technology called "LiveConnect." Unfortunately, this technique doesn't work with Internet Explorer. Listing 11.2 shows how JavaScript can get access to the default Toolkit to find out the user's window width, height, and resolution in dots per inch.

To use public Java methods in JavaScript:

1. sWidth = 0
   sHeight = 0
   sRes = 0

   This initializes our three variables, sWidth, sHeight, and sRes, to zero. Unlike Java, JavaScript uses loosely typed variables, which means that we don't need to explicitly declare them as integers, floats, or even numbers at all.

2. if (navigator.appName == "Netscape" &&
   → navigator.javaEnabled()) {

   Because LiveConnect is a Netscape-only technology, the following code will cause errors in other browsers. Consequently, there's a check here to make sure that only Netscape executes the following block of code. Also, we check to see if Java's enabled; there's no point in trying to access Java methods if we know that Java won't run in this browser.

3. defToolkit =
   → java.awt.Toolkit.getDefaultToolkit()

   Here we initialize a new variable, defToolkit, based on the Java method that gets Java's known information about the user's system.

Listing 11.2 How to get information about the user's setup without writing any Java

```
<HTML>
<HEAD>
 <TITLE>Listing 11.2</TITLE>
</HEAD>
<BODY BGCOLOR=WHITE>

 <SCRIPT LANGUAGE="JAVASCRIPT">
  <!-- Hide script from old browsers

  sWidth = 0
  sHeight = 0
  sRes = 0

  if (navigator.appName == "Netscape" &&
→ navigator.javaEnabled()) {
   defToolkit = java.awt.Toolkit.
    →getDefaultToolkit()
   sWidth = defToolkit.getScreenSize().width
   sHeight = defToolkit.getScreenSize().height
   sRes = defToolkit.getScreenResolution()
  }

  if (sWidth == 0 || sHeight == 0 || sRes == 0){
   sWidth = 640
   sHeight = 480
   sRes = 96
  }

  document.writeln("<H1>Your screen dimensions
→ are " + sWidth + " x " + sHeight + ", with a
→ resolution of " + sRes + " dpi.</H1>")

  // End hiding script from old browsers -->
 </SCRIPT>

</BODY>
</HTML>
```

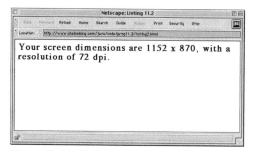

Figure 11.4 And here's what we've found out.

✔ Tips

■ This is a very useful piece of code when you're using JavaScript to open a window to the largest possible size. Given the screen height and width, JavaScript can open a new browser window to the correct dimensions to fill the user's screen.

■ Even though no Java applet is explicitly called, anyone running Netscape version 4 or later will see a message that says that Java is loading. LiveConnect has to start up Java in order to check the Toolkit.

4.   sWidth = defToolkit.getScreenSize().width
    sHeight = defToolkit.getScreenSize().
    → height

Given the default Toolkit, we can use the public Java method getScreenSize() to find out the height and width that the user's monitor supports.

5.   sRes = defToolkit.getScreenResolution()

Similarly, we can find out the screen resolution of the user's monitor by checking the public Java method getScreenResolution().

6.   }

The right curly brace closes the conditional code segment.

7.   if (sWidth == 0 || sHeight == 0 || sRes == 0)
   {

If any of the three variables we care about are still set to zero, then we want to execute the code following this if statement. This can happen if the user's browser wasn't Netscape, if the user is running with JavaScript on but Java off, or if there was an error of some type while accessing Java.

8.   sWidth = 640
    sHeight = 480
    sRes = 96

In this case, we want to set all the variables to their most likely value.

9.   }

And close the conditional.

10.   document.writeln("<H1>Your screen
    → dimensions are " + sWidth + " x " +
    → sHeight + ", with a resolution of →" +
    → sRes + " dpi.</H1>")

Here we use the JavaScript method document.writeln to print out our results, as shown in Figure 11.4.

Passing information from JavaScript to Java

We can also pass information between JavaScript and Java. Listing 11.3 and Applet 11.1 demonstrate how text entered into a JavaScript prompt window can be displayed in the browser window by Java.

To pass information from JavaScript to Java (JavaScript):

Listing 11.3 shows the JavaScript side of passing information to Java:

1. function startUp() {

    This begins a new JavaScript function called startUp().

2. document.myApplet.newText(prompt
    → ("What do you want to say?",""))

    Two things are happening here. First, the JavaScript prompt() method creates a new window, as shown in Figure 11.5. The first parameter passed to prompt() is the window's prompt, and the second parameter is the default input—in this case, nothing. The method prompt() returns a string, which will happen in Figure 11.6 when the user clicks on the OK button.

    The second thing is that we're calling the Java method newText(), which JavaScript knows by the name document.myApplet
    → .newText(). The parameter passed to this is the string returned by the JavaScript method prompt().

3. }

    This ends the startUp() function.

4. <BODY onLoad="startUp()" BGCOLOR=WHITE>

    This is a normal HTML BODY tag, with the addition of an onLoad handler. This event handler is triggered when the page is completely loaded. If the page were set up to call startUp() directly, it might try to call

Listing 11.3 Asks the user to enter a string...

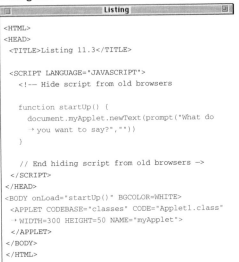

```
<HTML>
<HEAD>
 <TITLE>Listing 11.3</TITLE>

 <SCRIPT LANGUAGE="JAVASCRIPT">
  <!-- Hide script from old browsers

  function startUp() {
    document.myApplet.newText(prompt("What do
    → you want to say?",""))
  }

  // End hiding script from old browsers -->
 </SCRIPT>
</HEAD>
<BODY onLoad="startUp()" BGCOLOR=WHITE>
 <APPLET CODEBASE="classes" CODE="Applet1.class"
 → WIDTH=300 HEIGHT=50 NAME="myApplet">
 </APPLET>
</BODY>
</HTML>
```

Figure 11.5 The initial window in Internet Explorer (PC)

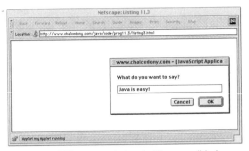

Figure 11.6 The same window in Netscape (Mac)

Applet 11.1 ...and then displays it on the screen.

```
Applet

import java.applet.*;
import java.awt.*;

public class Applet1 extends Applet {
  Font f = new Font("TimesRoman",Font.BOLD,36);
  String whatToSay;

  public void init() {
    setBackground(Color.white);
  }

  public void paint(Graphics g) {
    g.setFont(f);
    g.drawString(this.whatToSay, 100 , 25);
  }

  public void newText(String s) {
    this.whatToSay = s;
    repaint();
  }

}
```

Figure 11.7 And here's what the user sees.

the Java method newText() before the applet had completed loading. The onLoad event handler in the BODY tag allows us to be sure that everything on the page has completed loading.

5. <APPLET CODEBASE="classes" CODE="Applet1.
→ class" WIDTH=300 HEIGHT=50 NAME=
→ "myApplet">

This is again a normal HTML APPLET tag, with the addition of the NAME attribute. Giving the Java applet a name within HTML allows JavaScript to reference the applet, and thereby its public methods, as we did in step 2 above with document.my
→ Applet.newText().

To pass information from JavaScript to Java (Java):

Applet 11.1 shows the Java side of receiving information from JavaScript:

1. String whatToSay;

   This declares a string, whatToSay, for future use.

2. public void paint(Graphics g) {
       g.setFont(f);
       g.drawString(this.whatToSay, 100 , 25);
   }

   Whenever the Java applet needs to be painted, the string whatToSay will be drawn at position 100 x 25.

3. public void newText(String s) {
       this.whatToSay = s;
       repaint();
   }

   Whenever the method newText() is called by the JavaScript, it sets whatToSay to the passed parameter and forces a repaint() to update the applet window, as shown in Figure 11.7.

Passing information from Java to JavaScript

The previous pages showed an example in which JavaScript passed data to Java. In this example, JavaScript passes data to Java, and then Java passes the data right back to JavaScript, as shown in Figures 11.8 and 11.9.

To pass information from Java to JavaScript (JavaScript):

Listing 11.4 shows the JavaScript side of receiving information from Java:

1. function passCheck(passForm) {

We start by creating a new function, passCheck(). This function will check password entry fields, returning true if the password is valid, and false otherwise. The parameter that's being passed in, passForm, is the Form object on the HTML page.

2. goodPass = false

The content of the variable goodPass depends on whether or not the entered password is valid. We start by initializing it to false; i.e., the password is assumed to be bad.

3. if (passForm.pass.value != "") {

We only want to call the Java applet if the password entry field contains something. If it's blank, by definition it's bad, so why bother checking? The password field in the form is referred to as passForm.pass.value. To evaluate this, we start by looking at the Form object passForm, taking its text entry object called pass, and then looking at the value of that object. This notation illustrates one of the similarities between Java and JavaScript: Objects are identified by starting with the general and working towards the specific, using dot notation.

Figure 11.8 The password page in Netscape (Mac)

Figure 11.9 The password page in Internet Explorer (PC)

Listing 11.4 The user enters a password and clicks the Submit button...

```
<HTML>
<HEAD>
  <TITLE>Listing 11.4</TITLE>

  <SCRIPT LANGUAGE="JAVASCRIPT">
  <!-- Hide script from old browsers

    function passCheck(passForm) {
      goodPass = false
      if (passForm.pass.value != "") {
        goodPass = document.javaCheck.checkPass
        → (passForm.pass.value)
      }
      if (!goodPass) {
        alert("Invalid password")
        passForm.pass.focus()
        passForm.pass.select()
      }
      return goodPass
    }

    // End hiding script from old browsers -->
  </SCRIPT>

</HEAD>
<BODY BGCOLOR=WHITE>
  You'll have to enter the secret password to see
  → that page...<br>
  <FORM METHOD="post" ACTION=
  → "javascript:document.location=
  → 'http://www.chalcedony.com/java/'"
  → onSubmit="return passCheck(this)">
    Enter password: <INPUT TYPE="text"
    → NAME="pass"><br><br>
    <INPUT TYPE="submit" value="Submit">
  </FORM>

  <APPLET CODEBASE="classes" CODE="Applet2.class"
  → WIDTH=1 HEIGHT=1 NAME="javaCheck">
  </APPLET>
</BODY>
</HTML>
```

4.   goodPass = document.javaCheck.
        ⇢ checkPass(passForm.pass.value)

Here, goodPass is set to the value returned by the Java method checkPass() (which is discussed below). Again, the entered password is being referred to in the format passForm.pass.value, which is passed to checkPass().

5.   }

This right curly brace closes the conditional block.

6.   if (!goodPass) {

If the user didn't enter a valid password, we'll want to execute the following statements.

7.   alert("Invalid password")
        passForm.pass.focus()
        passForm.pass.select()

First, we put up a JavaScript alert window, letting the user know that their password just wasn't good enough. Next, we use the two JavaScript methods focus() and select(). The former puts the cursor into the chosen entry field, and the latter selects all the text in that field so that the user can automatically type over the existing entry.

8.   }

That's all we want to do if they entered an invalid password.

9.   return goodPass

Now goodPass is returned. It doesn't matter if the value is true or false, it just needs to be returned.

10.   }

And that's the end of the passCheck() function.

11.
```
<FORM METHOD="post" ACTION=
→ "javascript:document.location=
→ http://www.chalcedony.com/java/
→ "onSubmit="return passCheck(this)">
```

There are two pieces of JavaScript going on here. The ACTION attribute of the FORM tag is calling a line of JavaScript that will load a new page into the browser by resetting document.location to the desired URL.

The second piece of JavaScript is the onSubmit event handler. When the form is submitted, the passCheck() function is called. If the function returns false, the form submission is aborted, and the form's action never occurs. If passCheck() returns true, the action is allowed to proceed. The value this is passed to passCheck → (); as in Java, this implies the form currently being processed.

12.
```
<APPLET CODEBASE="classes" CODE=
→ "Applet2.class" WIDTH=1 HEIGHT=1
→ NAME="javaCheck">
```

This is a normal applet call, except that it's named (javaCheck) and it has a height and width both set to 1. While the applet does need to be on the page, there's no need for it to have a visible height and width, as this applet displays nothing on the screen.

To pass information from Java to JavaScript (Java):

Applet 11.2 shows the Java side of passing information to JavaScript:

1.
```
public boolean checkPass(String s) {
    return (s.equals("peachpit"));
}
```

This very simple Java method accepts a string as a parameter, and returns whether or not the passed string is equal to "peachpit". If it is, the value true is returned; if not, the value false is returned.

Applet 11.2 ...and this applet decides if it's valid.

```
import java.applet.*;

public class Applet2 extends Applet {

  public boolean checkPass(String s) {
    return (s.equals("peachpit"));
  }

}
```

✔ Tips

- A straightforward enhancement to this applet would be to change it to accept two strings: the one that the user entered and an encrypted target string. The Java applet could then take the first string, run it through a one-way encryption algorithm, and compare it to the second, returning true if they're the same. This would allow this applet to be used on any Web page, with the right algorithm making it impossible to break the password.

- In order to display the password in the figures, I've let it be seen in clear text. To make the password display as bullets, simply change the TYPE="text" attribute of the INPUT tag to TYPE="password".

TIC-TAC-TOE

While snippets of code are useful when you're learning how to do small things, it's not until you tie what you've learned together that Java applets really get impressive. This and the following chapters each take a fully realized Java applet and analyze what's going on in it step by step.

Playing a Java game of Tic-Tac-Toe

This applet plays a (not particularly good) game of Tic-Tac-Toe with a user. As you can see from the figures, it is possible for the player to beat the computer, unlike most other human versus computer versions of Tic-Tac-Toe which usually end in a tied game.

To play a game of Tic-Tac-Toe:

1. final static int moves[] = {4, 0, 2, 6, 8, 1, → 3, 5, 7};

First we creates an array named moves, which contains the given numbers. As it is declared final, the array can not change— i.e., it is a constant. This array determines which Tic-Tac-Toe square the computer will choose to take if neither player has a winning move. All of the possible moves are stored, in order of preference.

2. static boolean won[] = new boolean[1 << 9]; static final int DONE = (1 << 9) - 1;

Here two variables (one array and one int) are defined, both of which use the left shift operator for initialization. In both cases, this means that number 1 is shifted left 9 times (for the nine squares on the board), giving a result in binary of 1000000000 (1 followed by 9 zeros), which evaluates to 512 in decimal. Therefore, the array won consists of 512 Booleans (true/false values), and the int DONE is initialized to 512-1 or 511.

DONE could have been set explicitly to 511, but this approach keeps consistency with all the other places that need to identify separate squares.

3. static void isWon(int pos) {
    for (int i = 0 ; i < DONE ; i++) {
        if ((i & pos) == pos) {
            won[i] = true;

Listing 12.1

```
<html>
  <head>
  <base href="http://www.javasoft.com/applets/
  →TicTacToe/1.0.2/">
  <!-- modified by Chris Bucchere on 7/15/97 -->
  <title>TicTacToe v1.0</title>
  </head>
  <body>
    <h1>TicTacToe v1.0</h1>
    <hr>
    <applet code=TicTacToe.class width=120
    → height=120>
    alt="Your browser understands the &lt;
    → APPLET&gt; tag but isn't running the
    → applet, for some reason."
    Your browser is completely ignoring the
    → &lt;APPLET&gt; tag!
    </applet>
    <hr>
    Back to <a href="../../js-applets.html">
    →Applets from JavaSoft</a>.
    <hr>
    <a href="TicTacToe.java">The source.</a>
  </body>
</html>
```

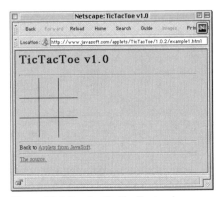

Figure 12.1 Running Tic-Tac-Toe in a browser brings up the applet.

Applet 12.1

```
/*
 * @(#)TicTacToe.java   1.4 96/12/06
 *
 * Copyright (c) 1994-1996 Sun Microsystems, Inc.
 * All Rights Reserved.
 *
 * Sun grants you ("Licensee") a non-exclusive,
 * royalty free, license to use,modify and
 * redistribute this software in source and
 * binary code form,provided that i) this
 * copyright notice and license appear on all
 * copies of the software; and ii) Licensee
 * does not utilize the software in a manner
 * which is disparaging to Sun.
 *
 * This software is provided "AS IS," without a
 * warranty of any kind. ALL EXPRESS OR IMPLIED
 * CONDITIONS, REPRESENTATIONS AND WARRANTIES,
 * INCLUDING ANY IMPLIED WARRANTY OF
 * MERCHANTABILITY, FITNES FOR A PARTICULAR
 * PURPOSE OR NON-INFRINGEMENT, ARE HEREBY
 * EXCLUDED. SUN AND ITS LICENSORS SHALL NOT BE
 * LIABLE FOR ANY DAMAGES SUFFERED BY LICENSEE
 * AS A RESULT OF USING, MODIFYING OR
 * DISTRIBUTING THE SOFTWARE OR IT DERIVATIVES
 * IN NO EVENT WILL SUN OR ITS
 * LICENSORS BE LIABLE FOR ANY LOST REVENUE,
 * PROFIT OR DATA, OR FOR DIRECT,INDIRECT,
 * SPECIAL, CONSEQUENTIAL, INCIDENTAL OR PUNITIVE
 * DAMAGES, HOWEVER CAUSED AND REGARDLESS OF THE
 * THEORY OF LIABILITY, ARISING OUT OF THE USE OF
 * OR INABILITY TO USE SOFTWARE, EVEN IF SUN HAS
 * BEEN ADVISED OF THEPOSSIBILITY OF SUCH
 * DAMAGES.
 *
 * This software is not designed or intended for
 * use in on-line control of aircraft, air
 * traffic, aircraft navigation or aircraft
 * communications; or in the design,
 * construction, operation or maintenance of
 * any nuclear facility. Licensee represents
 * and warrants  that it will not use or
 * redistribute the Software for such purposes.
 */

import java.awt.*;
import java.awt.image.*;
import java.net.*;
import java.applet.*;

/**
 * A TicTacToe applet. A very simple,
 * and mostly brain-dead implementation of your
 * favorite game! <p>
 *
 * In this game a position is represented by
 * a white and black bitmask. A bit is set if a
 * position is occupied. There are 9 squares so
 * there are 1<<9 possible positions for each
 * side. An array of 1<<9 booleans is created,
 * it mark sall the winning positions.
 *
```

Continued on next page

```
       }
     }
   }
```

This section and the next use the 512 bits in won to keep track of all the possible winning combinations.

4. static {
   isWon((1 << 0) | (1 << 1) | (1 << 2));
   isWon((1 << 3) | (1 << 4) | (1 << 5));
   isWon((1 << 6) | (1 << 7) | (1 << 8));
   isWon((1 << 0) | (1 << 3) | (1 << 6));
   isWon((1 << 1) | (1 << 4) | (1 << 7));
   isWon((1 << 2) | (1 << 5) | (1 << 8));
   isWon((1 << 0) | (1 << 4) | (1 << 8));
   isWon((1 << 2) | (1 << 4) | (1 << 6));
}

There are eight possible ways to win, as shown above. Each box is numbered from 0 to 8, so if one player has boxes 0, 1, and 2, for example, they've won. The call to isWon sets up the won array.

For example, if one player has squares 0, 1 and 2, they have the entire top row for a win. We take the value of 1 followed by the number of zero's equal to the square number. So, the first isWon() call could instead read isWon(1 | 10 | 100);.The "|" means to combine the three numbers together, with a one in any position that any of the three contain a one, with a result that the line could alternatively have been rewritten as isWon(7); (7 being the decimal equivalent of 111 in binary).The isWon() method is passed each of these values encoding a win, goes through the 512 possible positions for each side, and marks which ones are winning positions.

5. int bestMove(int white, int black) {
   int bestmove = -1;
   loop:
     for (int i = 0 ; i < 9 ; i++) {

Here the applet decides on its next move. There are nine boxes, so each has to be checked. The int i refers to the box we're checking, while bestmove is initialized to -1 to show that we haven't yet decided on the best possible move.

The white and black signify the computer and the player, respectively. They can't be referred to as X or O, as who goes first changes after each game.

6. int mw = moves[i];
   if (((white & (1 << mw)) == 0) && ((black &
   → (1 << mw)) == 0)) {

   The first line uses the moves array to get the best possible next move. The preferred position is the middle, then the top left, the top right, the bottom left, the bottom right, the top middle, the middle left, the middle right, and finally the bottom middle. The next line checks to see if this square is already taken. If so, there's no need to check it.

7. int pw = white | (1 << mw);
   if (won[pw]) {
       // white wins, take it!
       return mw;
   }

   The variable pw (possible white) is set for this move. Using the won array, the applet determines if this move would win the game for white; if so, the applet chooses it and ends the game.

8. for (int mb = 0 ; mb < 9 ; mb++) {
       if (((pw & (1 << mb)) == 0) && ((black &
       → (1 << mb)) == 0)) {
           int pb = black | (1 << mb);

   If there's no easy white move to win, we want to check to see if there's an easy black move to win that the suggested white move doesn't block. This code loops through the possible black moves.

PLAYING A JAVA GAME OF TIC-TAC-TOE

Applet 12.1 *continued*

```
                    Applet
* @version   1.2, 13 Oct 1995
* @author Arthur van Hoff
* @modified 96/04/23 Jim Hagen : winning
* sounds
*/
public class TicTacToe extends Applet {
  /**
  * White's current position. The computer is
  * white.
  */
  int white;

  /**
   * Black's current position. The user is black.
   */
  int black;

  /**
   * The squares in order of importance...
   */
  final static int moves[] = {4, 0, 2, 6, 8, 1, 3,
  → 5, 7};

  /**
   * The winning positions.
   */
  static boolean won[] = new boolean[1 << 9];
  static final int DONE = (1 << 9) - 1;
  static final int OK = 0;
  static final int WIN = 1;
  static final int LOSE = 2;
  static final int STALEMATE = 3;

  /**
   * Mark all positions with these bits set
   * as winning.
   */
  static void isWon(int pos) {
    for (int i = 0 ; i < DONE ; i++) {
      if ((i & pos) == pos) {
        won[i] = true;
      }
    }
  }

  /**
   * Initialize all winning positions.
   */
  static {
    isWon((1 << 0) | (1 << 1) | (1 << 2));
    isWon((1 << 3) | (1 << 4) | (1 << 5));
    isWon((1 << 6) | (1 << 7) | (1 << 8));
    isWon((1 << 0) | (1 << 3) | (1 << 6));
    isWon((1 << 1) | (1 << 4) | (1 << 7));
    isWon((1 << 2) | (1 << 5) | (1 << 8));
    isWon((1 << 0) | (1 << 4) | (1 << 8));
    isWon((1 << 2) | (1 << 4) | (1 << 6));
  }

  /**
   * Compute the best move for white.
```

Continued on next page

Applet 12.1 *continued*

```
============= Applet =============

 * @return the square to take
 */
int bestMove(int white, int black) {
  int bestmove = -1;

  loop:
  for (int i = 0 ; i < 9 ; i++) {
    int mw = moves[i];
    if (((white & (1 << mw)) == 0) && ((black &
   → (1 << mw)) == 0)) {
      int pw = white | (1 << mw);
      if (won[pw]) {
        // white wins, take it!
        return mw;
      }
      for (int mb = 0 ; mb < 9 ; mb++) {
        if (((pw & (1 << mb)) == 0) && ((black &
       → (1 << mb)) == 0)) {
          int pb = black | (1 << mb);
          if (won[pb]) {
            // black wins, take another
            continue loop;
          }
        }
      }
      // Neither white nor black can win in one
      // move, this will do.
      if (bestmove == -1) {
        bestmove = mw;
      }
    }
  }
  if (bestmove != -1) {
    return bestmove;
  }

  // No move is totally satisfactory, try the
  // first one that is open
  for (int i = 0 ; i < 9 ; i++) {
    int mw = moves[i];
    if (((white & (1 << mw)) == 0) && ((black &
   → (1 << mw)) == 0)) {
      return mw;
    }
  }

  // No more moves
  return -1;
}

/**
 * User move.
 * @return true if legal
 */
boolean yourMove(int m) {
  if ((m < 0) || (m > 8)) {
    return false;
  }
  if (((black | white) & (1 << m)) != 0) {
    return false;
  }
  black |= 1 << m;
```

Continued on next page

9.
```
if (won[pb]) {
    // black wins, take another
    continue loop;
}
```

If there's a possible black move to win, then we don't want to take the white move that we've been saving. The statement continue loop; returns the flow of control back up to the loop label and goes through the next iteration of the for loop checking for a better possible move.

10.
```
// Neither white nor black can win in one
→ move, this will do.
if (bestmove == -1) {
    bestmove = mw;
}
```

The code should only make it here if there are no possible moves that either white or black can make that would win the game. If this is true, we save the current candidate as bestmove.

11.
```
if (bestmove != -1) {
    return bestmove;
}
```

If bestmove has been set, then that's the one to take.

12.
```
// If no move is totally satisfactory, try the
→ first one that is open
for (int i = 0 ; i < 9 ; i++) {
    int mw = moves[i];
    if (((white & (1 << mw)) == 0) && ((black
   → & (1 << mw)) == 0)) {
        return mw;
    }
}
```

If the applet hasn't found a good move yet, it'll just take the preferred empty square.

13.
```
// No more moves
return -1;
```

If no moves are available, the game has ended in a stalemate.

14.
```
boolean yourMove(int m) {
    if ((m < 0) || (m > 8)) {
        return false;
    }
    if (((black | white) & (1 << m)) != 0) {
        return false;
    }
    black |= 1 << m;
    return true;
}
```

This checks to see if the move that the user entered is valid. If a square lower than 0 or greater than 8 was picked, it's an invalid move. Or, if that square was already taken, it's also an invalid move. Otherwise, we set that square to indicate that it was taken by black and return that the move was valid.

15.
```
boolean myMove() {
    if ((black | white) == DONE) {
        return false;
    }
    int best = bestMove(white, black);
    white |= 1 << best;
    return true;
}
```

Here's where the applet handles its move. If black or white is DONE, that means that there's a stalemate, so false is returned to show that there are no valid moves. Otherwise, we get the next move by calling bestMove, set white to show that that move has been taken, and return true.

16.
```
int status() {
    if (won[white]) {
        return WIN;
    }
    if (won[black]) {
        return LOSE;
    }
    if ((black | white) == DONE) {
        return STALEMATE;
    }
    return OK; }
```

Applet 12.1 *continued*

Applet

```
    return true;
}

/**
 * Computer move.
 * @return true if legal
 */
boolean myMove() {
    if ((black | white) == DONE) {
        return false;
    }
    int best = bestMove(white, black);
    white |= 1 << best;
    return true;
}

/**
 * Figure what the status of the game is.
 */
int status() {
    if (won[white]) {
        return WIN;
    }
    if (won[black]) {
        return LOSE;
    }
    if ((black | white) == DONE) {
        return STALEMATE;
    }
    return OK;
}

/**
 * Who goes first in the next game?
 */
boolean first = true;

/**
 * The image for white.
 */
Image notImage;

/**
 * The image for black.
 */
Image crossImage;

/**
 * Initialize the applet. Resize and load
 * images.
 */
public void init() {
    notImage = getImage(getCodeBase(),
    → "images/not.gif");
    crossImage = getImage(getCodeBase(),
    → "images/cross.gif");

}

/**
 * Paint it.
 */
```

Continued on next page

Applet 12.1 *continued*

```
public void paint(Graphics g) {
  Dimension d = size();
  g.setColor(Color.black);
  int xoff = d.width / 3;
  int yoff = d.height / 3;
  g.drawLine(xoff, 0, xoff, d.height);
  g.drawLine(2*xoff, 0, 2*xoff, d.height);
  g.drawLine(0, yoff, d.width, yoff);
  g.drawLine(0, 2*yoff, d.width, 2*yoff);

  int i = 0;
  for (int r = 0 ; r < 3 ; r++) {
    for (int c = 0 ; c < 3 ; c++, i++) {
      if ((white & (1 << i)) != 0) {
        g.drawImage(notImage, c*xoff + 1, r*yoff
        → + 1, this);
      }
      else if ((black & (1 << i)) != 0) {
        g.drawImage(crossImage, c*xoff + 1,
        → r*yoff + 1, this);
      }
    }
  }
}

/**
 * The user has clicked in the applet.
 * Figure out where and see if a legal move
 * is possible. If it is a legal move, respond
 * with a legal move (if possible).
 */
public boolean mouseUp(Event evt, int x, int y){
  switch (status()) {
    case WIN:
    case LOSE:
    case STALEMATE:
      play(getCodeBase(), "audio/return.au");
      white = black = 0;
      if (first) {
        white |= 1 << (int)(Math.random()
        → * 9);
      }
      first = !first;
      repaint();
      return true;
  }

  // Figure out the row/colum
  Dimension d = size();
  int c = (x * 3) / d.width;
  int r = (y * 3) / d.height;
  if (yourMove(c + r * 3)) {
    repaint();

    switch (status()) {
      case WIN:
        play(getCodeBase(), "audio/yahoo1.au");
        break;
      case LOSE:
        play(getCodeBase(), "audio/yahoo2.au");
        break;
      case STALEMATE:
        break;
```

Continued on next page

A call to status() returns the game's status. If white has won, WIN is returned; if black has wone, LOSE is returned. If black or white is DONE, STALEMATE is returned; otherwise, the game is in progress and the status is OK.

17.
```
Dimension d = size();
g.setColor(Color.black);
int xoff = d.width / 3;
int yoff = d.height / 3;
g.drawLine(xoff, 0, xoff, d.height);
g.drawLine(2*xoff, 0, 2*xoff,d.height);
g.drawLine(0, yoff, d.width, yoff);
g.drawLine(0, 2*yoff, d.width, 2*yoff);
```

The paint() method handles drawing the applet in the browser window. In this code, the applet gets the size of the applet area and divides it by three. Four lines are then drawn, dividing the area into thirds both horizontally and vertically.

18.
```
int i = 0;
for (int r = 0 ; r < 3 ; r++) {
  for (int c = 0 ; c < 3 ; c++, i++) {
    if ((white & (1 << i)) != 0) {
      g.drawImage(notImage,
      → c*xoff + 1, r*yoff + 1, this);
    }
    else if ((black & (1 << i)) != 0) {
      g.drawImage(crossImage,
      → c*xoff + 1, r*yoff + 1, this);
    }
  }
}
```

In the remainder of the paint() method, the Xs and Os are drawn. The r loop counts rows and the c loop counts columns. In each square that white has claimed, an O is drawn, and in each square that black has claimed, an X is drawn.

19.
```
switch (status()) {
    case WIN:
    case LOSE:
    case STALEMATE:
        play(getCodeBase(), "audio/
        → return.au");
        white = black = 0;
        if (first) {
            white |= 1 << (int)(Math.
            → random() * 9);
        }
        first = !first;
        repaint();
        return true;
}
```

The mouseUp() method handles the main event check in this applet. If the game has already come to a conclusion and the user clicks the mouse in the playing area, a new game is started. Any result of status() other than OK causes a sound to play and white and black to be set to unplayed. If it's now white's (the applet's) turn to go first, white is set to a random square. Then, the variable first is reset to keep track of who will go first next time, and repaint() is called to clear the playing board.

20.
```
// Figure out the row/column
Dimension d = size();
int c = (x * 3) / d.width;
int r = (y * 3) / d.height;
if (yourMove(c + r * 3)) {
    repaint();
```

If it's the user's turn to go first, the applet needs to handle their move. The placement of the mouseUp needs to be calculated and then checked for validity. If it's valid, the applet is repainted with the user's new X.

21.
```
switch (status()) {
    case WIN:
        play(getCodeBase(), "audio/
        → yahoo1.au");
        break;
    case LOSE:
```

Applet 12.1 *continued*

```
Applet

            default:
                if (myMove()) {
                    repaint();
                switch (status()) {
                case WIN:
                    play(getCodeBase(), "audio/yahoo1
                    → .au");
                    break;
                case LOSE:
                    play(getCodeBase(), "audio/yahoo2
                    → .au");
                    break;
                case STALEMATE:
                    break;
                default:
                    play(getCodeBase(), "audio/ding.au");
                }
            }
            else {
                play(getCodeBase(), "audio/beep.au");
            }
        }
    }
    else {
        play(getCodeBase(), "audio/beep.au");
    }
    return true;
}

public String getAppletInfo() {
    return "TicTacToe by Arthur van Hoff";
}
}
```

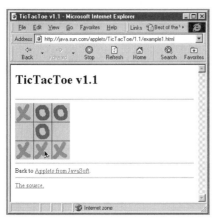

Figure 12.2 After looking at the code, you know what the applet's strategies are.

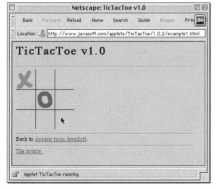

Figure 12.3 So then it's easy to play winning games…

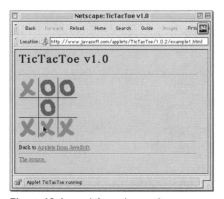

Figure 12.4 …and if you choose, the same winning games over and over again.

```
            play(getCodeBase(), "audio/
       → yahoo2.au");
            break;
         case STALEMATE:
            break;
```

Now that the user has made their move, status() is once again checked. If the result is a win or loss, a sound congratulating the winner is played (the winning sound is much more enthusiastic than the losing sound).

22.
```
default:
   if (myMove()) {
      repaint();
```

In the default case, the game is still in progress, so the computer takes its turn by calling myMove() and repainting the window.

23.
```
switch (status()) {
   case WIN:
      play(getCodeBase(), "audio/
   → yahoo1.au");
      break;
   case LOSE:
      play(getCodeBase(), "audio/
   → yahoo2.au");
      break;
   case STALEMATE:
      break;
   default:
      play(getCodeBase(), "audio/
   → ding.au");
```

Now that the computer has taken its turn, it's time to check status() again. The only difference between this and the code above in step 21 is that here when the code falls into the default block, a sound plays to tell the user that it's now their turn.

✔ Tip

- Both "|" and "||" are valid Java operators, as are "&" and "&&". The doubled versions are logical operators: you can set hasPet to be if a person has a cat or a dog, or you can set isGeek to be if a person who has both a pocket protector *and* a propeller beanie (and yes, I know where both of mine are). The single versions operate only on numbers, which are then internally converted to their binary values (that is, all 1's and 0's) and compared character by character, resulting in a binary combination of the numbers.

A SIMPLE
CALCULATOR

This simple applet puts a small calculator on a user's Web page.

A Simple Calculator

This applet gives you the functionality of a simple four-function calculator (plus a little extra) and the framework to add your own keys. Start with Applet 13.1, calculator.java, and just expand the size of the grid, add your new buttons, and add handlers in the calc() method. That's all there is to it!

To build a simple Java calculator:

1. setBackground(Color.white);
   display = new TextField("0",6);
   display.setEditable(false);
   add(display);

   In this initialization code, we start by changing the applet's background to white to blend in with the page. Then we add the calculator's display field, giving it an initialized display of zero and setting it to not be editable.

2. Panel p = new Panel();
   p.setLayout(new GridLayout(5, 4));

   Next, we create a new panel for the buttons, which will go into a 5 by 4 GridLayout.

3. for (int i = 1; i <= 9; i++) {
       p.add(new Button("" + I));
       if (i==3)
           p.add(new Button("+"));
       if (i==6)
           p.add(new Button("-"));
   }

   The numbers 1 through 9 are then added in three rows. The final button at the end of each row is one of the main functions, so they end up in a neat column, as shown in Figures 13.1 and 13.2.

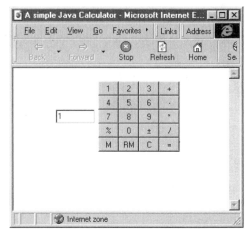

Figure 13.1 The calculator as seen in Internet Explorer for Windows 95

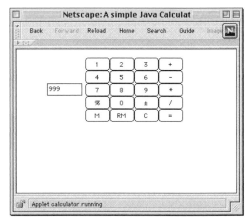

Figure 13.2 The calculator as seen in Netscape for the Mac

Applet 13.1 A simple Java calculator

```java
import java.awt.*;
import java.applet.*;

public class calculator extends Applet {
  TextField display;
  int saveNum = 0;
  int memNum = 0;
  char op = '=';
  char lastOp = '=';
  boolean newNum = true;

  public void init() {
    setBackground(Color.white);

    display = new TextField("0",6);
    display.setEditable(false);
    add(display);

    Panel p = new Panel();
    p.setLayout(new GridLayout(5, 4));
    for (int i = 1; i <= 9; i++) {
      p.add(new Button("" + i));
      if (i==3)
        p.add(new Button("+"));
      if (i==6)
        p.add(new Button("-"));
    }
    p.add(new Button("*"));
    p.add(new Button("%"));
    p.add(new Button("0"));
    p.add(new Button("±"));
    p.add(new Button("/"));
    p.add(new Button("M"));
    p.add(new Button("RM"));
    p.add(new Button("C"));
    p.add(new Button("="));
    add(p);
  }

  public boolean action(Event evt, Object arg) {
    if (arg instanceof String) {
      String s = (String) arg;
      if (s.charAt(0) >= '0' && s.charAt(0) <=
 '9') {
        if (newNum)
          display.setText(s);
        else
          display.setText(display.getText() + s);
        newNum = false;
      }
      else {
        if (s.charAt(0) == '-' && newNum) {
          display.setText("-");
        newNum = false;
        }
        else {
          op = s.charAt(0);
          calc (Integer.parseInt(display
 getText()));
          newNum = true;
```

Applet 13.1 *Continued*

```java
        }
        lastOp = op;
      }
      return true;
    }
    return super.action(evt, arg);
  }

  public void calc(int n) {
    switch (op) {
      case '+':
      case '-':
      case '*':
      case '/':
      case '%':
        saveNum = n;
        return;
    }

    if (op == '=')
      op = lastOp;

    switch (op) {
      case '+':
        saveNum += n;
        break;
      case '-':
        saveNum -= n;
        break;
      case '*':
        saveNum *= n;
        break;
      case '/':
        saveNum /= n;
        break;
      case '%':
        saveNum %= n;
        break;
      case 'M':
        memNum = n;
        saveNum = n;
        break;
      case 'R':
        saveNum = memNum;
        break;
      case 'C':
        saveNum = 0;
        break;
      case '±':
        saveNum = -n;
        break;
    }
    display.setText("" + saveNum);
  }
}
```

4. p.add(new Button("*"));
p.add(new Button("%"));
p.add(new Button("0"));
p.add(new Button("±"));
p.add(new Button("/"));
p.add(new Button("M"));
p.add(new Button("RM"));
p.add(new Button("C"));
p.add(new Button("="));
add(p);

Then the rest of the buttons are added one by one, in the order we choose. The ± key changes the sign, the M key stores the current value in memory, the RM key recalls the saved memory, and the C key clears the display by resetting it to 0. The panel is then added, and that's all for the init() method.

5. if (arg instanceof String) {

Inside the action() method, the only type of events we need to handle are those involving strings (i.e., the buttons we created). Otherwise, Java can handle them just fine with its default behavior.

6. String s = (String) arg;
if (s.charAt(0) >= '0' && s.charAt(0)<= '9') {

If the string caught by the event handler is a character between 0 and 9, then the user must have clicked on a number key.

7. if (newNum)
     display.setText(s);
else display.setText(display.getText() + s);
newNum = false;

The Boolean variable newNum tells the applet whether or not the number being entered should overwrite the existing value. For instance, if the display currently contains 0 and the user is trying to enter the number 15, we want newNum to start off as true. In this case, clicking on the 1 key will overwrite the 0. However, when the user clicks on the 5 key, we want the 5 appended to the 1 to display the desired result. Consequently, as soon as one good number has been entered, newNum is set to false.

8.
```
if (s.charAt(0) == '-' && newNum) {
    display.setText("-");
    newNum = false;
}
```

If the key pressed was non-numeric, we start to handle it here. In this section, if the user clicked on the - (dash) key before typing in a number, we assume that they want to enter a negative number. In this case, we put the - in the display and turn off newNum to end the overwriting.

9.
```
op = s.charAt(0);
calc (Integer.parseInt(display.getText()));
newNum = true;
```

If we make it to this section, the user clicked on an operator that needs to be handled. The operator is stored in op, and the calc() method (explained below) is called with a parameter set to the integer value of the display field. When this is complete, the newNum flag is set back to true, so that the next number entered will again write over the contents of the display field.

10.
```
        lastOp = op;
    }
    return true;
}
return super.action(evt, arg);
```

When we've completed handling the operator, the last operator chosen is saved in lastOp. Then, if the applet has successfully completed handling the event, we return with a value of true. If the event trapped wasn't a string event, we let Java handle it by calling the super.action() method.

11.
```
public void calc(int n) {
    switch (op) {
        case '+':
```

```
    case '-':
    case '*':
    case '/':
    case '%':
        saveNum = n;
        return;
}
```

Here's the meat of the applet: the calc() method, where the actual work is done. There are two types of operators: unary, which operates on one number, and binary, which requires two numbers. With binary operators, no calculation is actually done until both numbers have been entered. So here we handle the 5 binary operators by saving the number currently in the display field. The operator being processed will be saved by the calling method.

12.
```
if (op == '=')
    op = lastOp;
```

If the user clicked on the = (equals) key, we should now have enough information to handle the last operator entered.

13.
```
switch (op) {
    case '+':
        saveNum += n;
        break;
    case '-':
        saveNum -= n;
        break;
    case '*':
        saveNum *= n;
        break;
    case '/':
        saveNum /= n;
        break;
    case '%':
        saveNum %= n;
        break;
```

These five cases are virtually identical. In each case, the applet takes the number saved in step 11 above, the current value of the display field, and the operator entered between them to update the display field.

14. case 'M':
```
    memNum = n;
    saveNum = n;
    break;
```

When the user chooses to store the display field in memory, nothing appears to happen on the screen but the applet stores the current value in memNum.

15. case 'R':
```
    saveNum = memNum;
    break;
```

When the user then chooses to retrieve this number, we simply set saveNum to memNum to redisplay the stored value.

16. case 'C':
```
    saveNum = 0;
    break;
```

To clear the display field, we zero out saveNum.

17. case '±':
```
    saveNum = -n;
    break;
```

To change the sign of the number in the display field, we set saveNum to the negative value of the current display field. This will set positive numbers to their negative values, and negative numbers to their positive values.

18. display.setText("" + saveNum);

The last step is to display the number as modified by the operator the user chose.

Now, add your own buttons to the calculator by changing the size of the grid and adding new handlers to the calc() method.

HIERARCHICAL MENU

HIERARCHICAL MENU

A common use of Java on Web sites is to display a hierarchical menu, that is, a menu that displays a list of submenus when the cursor is moved over it. This applet, written by Patrick Chan for Sun Microsystems, can be found along with his other applets at http://www.xeo.com.

Java Hierarchical Menu

A hierarchical menu allows you to use both a menu and a submenu within a limited area on your Web page, as shown in Figures 14.1, 14.2, and 14.3. This applet (Applet 14.1) gets the menu information from the calling HTML file in Listing 14.1, which allows a single applet to be used by multiple pages with different menus.

Figure 14.1 The hierarchical menu as it appears when the page is first loaded—at first, it looks just like a normal menu...

To create a hierarchical menu:

1. image = getImage(getCodeBase(),
   → getParameter("image"));

   First we read the name of the image from the calling HTML file, then load the image itself. For the name and associated value of this and the following parameters, see Table 14.1 at the end of this chapter.

2. marginH = Integer.parseInt(getParameter
   → ("marginh"));
   marginV = Integer.parseInt(getParameter
   → ("marginv"));

   Then we read in the marginh and marginv values from the HTML file.

Figure 14.2 ...until the user moves the cursor over a field, possibly expecting to see just a simple rollover...

3. ints = parseInt(getParameter("bg-color"),
   → " ");
   bgColor = new Color(ints[0], ints[1],
   → ints[2]);

   The applet uses five color fields, each defined by a set of three numbers (red, green, and blue values), which can be anywhere from 0 to 255. This format allows for over 16 million different colors. The array ints gets the three values, and then the Color() method turns those numbers into a Java color. This same code is then repeated for each of the four other color fields.

Figure 14.3 ...but instead, more options magically appear.

4. bbuf = createImage(size().width, size().
   → height);
   bbufG = bbuf.getGraphics();

Figure 14.4 This is what the menu graphic looks like, under the hood.

Table 14.2

Menu parameters	
PARAMETER	**DESCRIPTION**
downUp	A parameter specifying whether the menu should be drawn downward or upward from dstPt.
dstPt	A set of two numbers specifying the location on the image where srcImage should appear. The two numbers are x and y.
hotbox	A set of four numbers specifying a rectangle on the image. When the cursor rolls into the hotbox, a menu is displayed. The four numbers are x, y, width, and height.
label	The menu label; it can appear on more than one line by using the newline parameter described above.
mainURL	The URL that the applet will send the browser to when the user clicks in the hotbox.
srcImage	A set of four numbers specifying a rectangle on the image. When the cursor rolls into the hotbox, the sub-image defined by srcImage is drawn over the main image. The location is defined by dstPt. The four numbers are - x, y, width, and height.
url	The URL that the applet will send the browser to when the user clicks on the menu item.

This creates a buffer area for double-buffering the menu graphic.

5.
```
int fh = Integer.parseInt(getParameter
  → ("font-height"));
int i = fh;
```

Here we read in the font height and save it for future use.

6.
```
while (i > 10) {
    f = new Font(getParameter("font"),
      → Font.PLAIN, i);
    fm = getFontMetrics(f);
    if (fm.getHeight() <= fh) {
        break;
    }
    i--;
}
```

We need to calculate the actual font size based on the font height. This code loops around, checking to see if a font of this size has the height requested. If so, we exit the loop using break. Otherwise, we subtract 1 from the font size and try again.

7.
```
for (i=0; ; i++) {
    if (getParameter("menu"+i)==null) {
        hitArea = new Rectangle[i];
        srcRect = new Rectangle[i];
        dstPt = new Point[i];
        url = new String[i];
        down = new boolean[i];
        itemUrl = new String[i][];
        item = new String[i][];
        break;
    }
}
```

This loop counts the number of menuX parameters being passed by the calling HTML file, then creates new arrays of the required size.

8.
```
for (i=0; i<hitArea.length; i++) {
```

For each menuX parameter in the calling HTML file, the applet will execute the code in steps 9 and 10.

9. String[] fields = parse(getParameter
→ ("menu"+i), getParameter("separator"));
ints = parseInt(fields[0], " ");
hitArea[i] = new Rectangle(ints[0], ints[1],
→ ints[2], ints[3]);
ints = parseInt(fields[1], " ");
srcRect[i] = new Rectangle(ints[0], ints[1],
→ ints[2], ints[3]);
ints = parseInt(fields[2], " ");
dstPt[i] = new Point(ints[0], ints[1]);
down[i] = fields[3].equals("d");
url[i] = fields[4];
item[i] = new String[(fields.length-5)/2];
itemUrl[i] = new String[(fields.length-5)/2];

We read in each of the menuX parameters,
as described in Table 14.2.

10. for (int j=0; j<item [i].length; j++) {
item[i][j] = fields[j*2+5];
itemUrl[i][j] = fields[j*2+6];
}

For each item in each menuX parameter,
we set the item and itemURL arrays.

11. String[] parse(String s, String sep) {

This creates a new method, parse(),
which is passed two strings: The first is
the string to parse, and the second is a
separator used to define how the first
should be parsed. In other words, if the
two strings passed are "a|b|c" and "|",
the pipe character ("|") is used to split
up the first string, with the result being
an array consisting of three strings: "a",
"b", and "c".

12. StringTokenizer st = new StringTokenizer
→ (s, sep);
String result[] =
→ new String[st.countTokens()];

The variable st is set to the number of
strings that will be returned by calling
the StringTokenizer() method. Then, given
st, the result array is created with the
correct length.

Listing 14.1

```
┌─────────────────── Applet ───────────────────┐
<HTML>
<HEAD>
 <TITLE>XEO MENU</TITLE>
</HEAD>
<BODY BGCOLOR=WHITE>
<APPLET CODEBASE="." CODE="XeoMenu" WIDTH=160
 ›HEIGHT=364>
<PARAM NAME=bg-color value="255 255 255">
<PARAM NAME=image VALUE="menu.gif">
<PARAM NAME=separator VALUE="|">
<PARAM NAMe=n   ˙ e VALUE="^">
<PARAM NAME=fc .t VALUE="Helvetica">
<PARAM ﾗ ﾉME=font-height VALUE="14">
<PARA.ﾗ NAME=marginh VALUE=2>
<PARAM NAME=marginv VALUE=2>
<param name=fg-menu-color value="0 0 0">
<param name=bg-menu-color value="255 255 255">
<param name=fg-hi-menu-color value="0 0 0">
<param name=bg-hi-menu-color value="150 150 150">

<PARAM NAME=menu0 VALUE="0 0 150 24|150 0 150
 → 24|0 0|d|chap01.html|Cans &
Can'ts|chap011.html|Secure Sandbox|chap012.html">
<PARAM NAME=menu1 VALUE="0 24 150 24|150 24 150
 → 24|0
24|d|chap02.html|OO|chap021.html|Applet|chap022.
 →html|Glossary|chap023.html">
<PARAM NAME=menu2 VALUE="0 53 150 34|150 53 150
 → 34|0 53|d|chap03.html|Calling Java|chap031.
 →html|Displaying HTML|chap023.html|Placing
 →Applets|chap033.html|Passing Params|chap034.
 →html">
<PARAM NAME=menu3 VALUE="0 86 150 24|150 86 150
 → 24|0 86|d|chap04.html|Hello World!|chap041.html
 →|Changing^Font Face|chap042.html|Setting back-
 →^ground color|chap043.html|HTML to Java|chap044
 →.html|Adding comments|chap045.html|Font styles
 →|chap046.html|Font colors|chap047.html">
<PARAM NAME=menu4 VALUE="0 111 150 24|150 111 150
 →24|0 111|d|chap05.html|Declaring^variables|
 →chap051.html|Strings|chap052.html|Variable
 → scope|chap053.html|String methods|chap054.html|
 →Numbers|chap055.html|String^conversions|chap056
 →.html|Numeric^conversions|chap057.html|
 →Conversion^by casting|chap058.html|Arrays|
 →chap059.html">
<PARAM NAME=menu5 VALUE="0 139 150 30|150 139 150
 →30|0 139|d|chap06.html|If/then|chap061.html|
 →If/then/else|chap062.html|For loops|chap063
 →.html|While loops|chap064.html|Do/while loops|
 →chap065.html|Break &^Continue|chap066.html|
 →Switch/Case|chap067.html">
<PARAM NAME=menu6 VALUE="0 175 150 30|150 175 150
30|0 175|u|chap07.html|Drawing lines|chap071.html
 →|2 Dimensions|chap072.html|Freehand drawing|
 →chap073.html|Capturing keys|chap074.html|Arrow
keys|chap075.html|Varying speed|chap076.html">
```

Continued on next page

Listing 14.1 *continued*

```
Applet

<PARAM NAME=menu7 VALUE="0 209 150 24|150 209 150
→24|0 209|d|chap08.html|Password^protection|
→chap081.html|Text fields|chap082.html|
→Checkboxes|chap083.html|Radio buttons|chap084
→.html|Pulldown menus|chap085.html|On-the-fly
menus|chap086.html|Text areas|chap087.html|
→Lists|chap088.html">
<PARAM NAME=menu8 VALUE="0 236 150 24|150 236 150
→24|0 236|d|chap09.html|No Layout|chap091.html|
→FlowLayout|chap092.html|More FlowLayout|chap093
→.html|Border Layout|chap094.html|Grid Layout|
→chap095.html|Insets|chap096.html|Panels|chap097
→.html|CardLayout|chap098.html|GridBagLayout|
→chap099.html">
<PARAM NAME=menu9 VALUE="0 264 150 30|150 264 150
→30|0 264|d|chap10.html|Java animation|chap101
→.html|Threading|chap102.html|Double-buffering|
→chap103.html">
<PARAM NAME=menu10 VALUE="0 296 150 30|150 296
→150 30|0 296|d|chap11.html|Checking on Java|
→chap111.html|Public Java methods|chap112.html|
→JavaScript to Java|chap113.html|Using Java
→methods|chap114.html">
<PARAM NAME=menu11 VALUE="0 325 150 30|150 325
→150 30|0 325|d|chap12.html|Tic-Tac-Toe|
→chap12.html|Calculator|chap13.html|Hierarchical
→^Menu|chap14.html">

</APPLET>
</BODY>
</HTML>
```

13. for (int i=0; i<result.length; i++) {
        result[i] = st.nextToken();
      }
      return result;

This loop sets the result array, and then we return result to end the method.

14. int[] parseInt(String s, String sep) {

This method is similar to parse(), except that the first string is a list of integers, so the result is an array of ints.

15. StringTokenizer st = new StringTokenizer
      → (s, sep);
      int[] result = new int[st.countTokens()];

Again, the StringTokenizer() method is used to break apart the input string, and a result array is declared.

16. for (int i=0; i<result.length; i++) {
        result[i] =
        → Integer.parseInt(st.nextToken());
      }

Here, the result array is set based on the parsed input string.

17. public void paint(Graphics g) {
        imageDone = false;
        update(g);
      }

The overridden paint() method does just two simple things: It resets imageDone to false and then calls the update() method.

18. public void update(Graphics g) {
        Graphics g2;
        if (!imageDone) {
          imageDone = g.drawImage(image, 0, 0,
          → this);
          return;
        }

We want to make sure that the menu image is completely loaded before displaying it on-screen. Here, we check to see if the menu image has been loaded; if not, drawImage() is called.

19. bbufG.setColor(bgColor);
bbufG.fillRect(0, 0, size().width, size().
→ height);
bbufG.drawImage(image, 0, 0, this);

The buffer is filled with the chosen background color, and then the menu image is drawn in the buffer.

20. if (curMenu >= 0) {

The variable curMenu contains the current menu item that the cursor is pointing to. If curMenu is nonzero, then we want to draw the hierarchical submenu.

21. g2 = bbuf.getGraphics();
g2.clipRect(dstPt[curMenu].x, dstPt
→ [curMenu].y, srcRect[curMenu].width,
→ srcRect[curMenu].height);
g2.drawImage(image, dstPt[curMenu].
→ x-srcRect[curMenu].x, dstPt[curMenu].
→ y-srcRect[curMenu].y, this);
g2.dispose();
g2 = bbuf.getGraphics();

Now we paint the overlay image.

22. for (int i=0; i<menuItemRect.length; i++) {
drawMenuItem(g2, i);
}

For each line in the submenu, we call the drawMenuItem() method.

23. g2.dispose();
}
g.drawImage(bbuf, 0, 0, this);

Then we finish off setting up the submenu and display it on the screen.

24. void drawMenuItem(Graphics g, int i) {

This creates the drawMenuItem() method, which handles creating and drawing the submenus.

25. String[] line = parse(item[curMenu][i],
getParameter("newline"));

We get the newline character from the calling HTML file.

Applet 14.1

```
/*
  Copyright: Sun Microsystems 1997.  All rights
  →reserved.
  Author: Patrick Chan (www.xeo.com)   7/19/96
  Version: 1.1
*/

import java.applet.*;
import java.awt.*;
import java.util.*;
import java.net.*;

public class XeoMenu extends Applet {
  // The background image.  This had better not be
  → null.
  Image image;

  // These two fields are used to do double-
  →buffering.
  // The dimensions of bbuf is exactly the
  → dimensions of the applet.
  Image bbuf;
  Graphics bbufG;

  // This field is set to true only when the
  →background image has
  // completely loaded.
  boolean imageDone;

  /* Menu data */
  Rectangle[] hitArea;
  Rectangle[] srcRect;
  Point[] dstPt;
  boolean[] down;
  String[] url;

  /* Submenu data */
  String[][] itemUrl;
  String[][] item;

  // If >= 0, this fields holds the index of the
  → current menu.
  // If -1, no menu is current.
  int curMenu;

  // If >= 0, this fields holds the index of the
  → current menu item.
  // If -1, no menu item is current.
  int curMenuItem;

  // This is an array of rectangles - one
  → rectangle for each menu item.
  // Each rectangle specifies the
  // location (relative to the left-corner of the
  → applet) of a menu item.
  //
  // menuItemRect is null when curMenu is -1.
  // It becomes non-null when curMenu >= 0.
  //
  → to define classes for
  // the menu and menu items.  However, I decided
  → for this little applet
```

Continued on next page

Applet 14.1 *continued*

```
                    Applet

// to keep the number of class files to a
→ minimum to minimize the download
// time.
Rectangle[] menuItemRect;

// This is the color to paint "behind" the
→ image.
Color bgColor;

// [0] is the text color of a menu item; [1] is
→ the text color of a highlighted
// menu item.
Color fgMenuColor[] = new Color[2];

// This is the background of a menu item; [1] is
→ the background color of a
// highlighted menu item.
Color bgMenuColor[] = new Color[2];

// marginH is the number of pixels on the left
→ and right edges of the menu.
// marginV is the number of pixels on the top
→ and bottom edges of the menu.
int marginH, marginV;

// This is the font used to display the menu
→ item labels.
Font f;

// This is the font metrics of 'f'.
FontMetrics fm;

public void init() {
  int[] ints;

  // Grab applet parameters.
  image = getImage(getCodeBase(),
  → getParameter("image"));
  marginH =
  → Integer.parseInt(getParameter("marginh"));
  marginV =
  → Integer.parseInt(getParameter("marginv"));

  // Get color parameters.
  ints = parseInt(getParameter("bg-color"),
  → " ");
  bgColor = new Color(ints[0], ints[1],
  → ints[2]);
  ints = parseInt(getParameter("fg-menu-color"),
  → " ");
  fgMenuColor[0] = new Color(ints[0], ints[1],
  → ints[2]);
  ints = parseInt(getParameter("fg-hi-menu-
  → color"), " ");
  fgMenuColor[1] = new Color(ints[0], ints[1],
  → ints[2]);
  ints = parseInt(getParameter("bg-menu-color"),
  → " ");
  bgMenuColor[0] = new Color(ints[0], ints[1],
  → ints[2]);
  ints = parseInt(getParameter("bg-hi-menu-
  → color"), " ");
```

Continued on next page

26. int hi = 0;
if (i == curMenuItem) {
  hi = 1;
  getAppletContext().showStatus(itemUrl
  → [curMenu][i]);
}

If the submenu item that we're currently processing is the same menu item that the cursor is currently on, we call showStatus() to display the URL in the browser's status area, and set the highlight variable hi to 1.

27. g.setColor(bgMenuColor[hi]);
g.fillRect(menuItemRect[i].x, menuItem
→ Rect[i].y, menuItemRect[i].width,
→ menuItemRect[i].height);

These lines set the background color based on hi and fill the rectangle with that color.

28. g.setColor(fgMenuColor[hi]);
g.drawRect(menuItemRect[i].x, menuItem
→ Rect[i].y, menuItemRect[i].width, menu
→ ItemRect[i].height);

These lines set the color for the text and box, and draw a box around the menu item.

29. g.setFont(f);
y = menuItemRect[i].y + marginV;

These lines set the font and initialize the y-placement of the text.

30. for (i=0; i<line.length; i++) {

This is a loop, because there may be more than one line for a single submenu item.

31. g.drawString(line[i], menuItemRect[i].
→ x+menuItemRect[i].width-fm.string
→ Width(line[i])-marginH, y + fm.
→ getAscent());y += fm.getHeight();

Here we draw the submenu text at the correct location, and increment the y-location for the next line.

32. public boolean mouseExit(Event evt, int x,
→ int y) {
   curMenuItem = curMenu = -1;
   repaint();
   return true;
}

The mouseExit event is triggered when the cursor leaves the menu area. In this case, the cursor isn't over a menu option anymore, so curMenuItem and curMenu are both set to -1, and the applet is repainted.

33. public boolean mouseEnter(Event evt, int x,
→ int y) {
   return mouseMove(evt, x, y);
}

If the mouse moves back onto the menu area, we force a mouseMove event to be triggered.

34. public boolean mouseDown(Event evt, int x,
→ int y) {
   try {

The mouseDown event is triggered when the user holds a mouse button down while the cursor is over the menu.

35. String u = null;
if (curMenuItem >= 0 && itemUrl[curMenu].
→ length > 0) {
   u = itemUrl[curMenu][curMenuItem];
}

If the user has triggered the mouseDown event over an area where there's an active submenu URL, we set u to that URL.

36. else
   if (curMenu >= 0) {
     u = url[curMenu];
   }

Otherwise, we set u to the generic URL for that menu item.

37. if (u != null) {
   URL url = new URL(getDocumentBase(),
   → u);

Applet 14.1 *continued*

```
bgMenuColor[1] = new Color(ints[0], ints[1],
→ ints[2]);

// Create back buffer for double-buffering.
bbuf = createImage(size().width,
→ size().height);
bbufG = bbuf.getGraphics();

// Determine the font from the font-height.
int fh = Integer.parseInt(getParameter("font-
→ height"));
int i = fh;
while (i > 10) {
  f = new Font(getParameter("font"),
→ Font.PLAIN, i);
  fm = getFontMetrics(f);
  if (fm.getHeight() <= fh) {
   break;
  }
  i--;
}

// Get the menu parameters.
for (i=0; ; i++) {
  if (getParameter("menu"+i) == null) {
   hitArea = new Rectangle[i];
   srcRect = new Rectangle[i];
   dstPt = new Point[i];
   url = new String[i];
   down = new boolean[i];
   itemUrl = new String[i][];
   item = new String[i][];

   break;
  }
}

for (i=0; i<hitArea.length; i++) {
  String[] fields = parse(getParameter
→ ("menu"+i), getParameter("separator"));

  // Get the hit area.
  ints = parseInt(fields[0], " ");
  hitArea[i] = new Rectangle(ints[0], ints[1],
→ ints[2], ints[3]);

  // Get the source image.
  ints = parseInt(fields[1], " ");
  srcRect[i] = new Rectangle(ints[0], ints[1],
→ ints[2], ints[3]);

  // Get the destination point.
  ints = parseInt(fields[2], " ");
  dstPt[i] = new Point(ints[0], ints[1]);
  down[i] = fields[3].equals("d");
  url[i] = fields[4];

  item[i] = new String[(fields.length-5)/2];
  itemUrl[i] = new String[(fields.length-
→ 5)/2];
  for (int j=0; j<item[i].length; j++) {
   item[i][j] = fields[j*2+5];
```

Continued on next page

Applet 14.1 *continued*

```
|  Applet                                    |

      itemUrl[i][j] = fields[j*2+6];
    }
  }
}


// s is a string containing 'sep' separators.
→ This method
// breaks up the string at the separators and
→ returns the resulting
// strings in an array.  The result may have
→ zero length but is never null.
String[] parse(String s, String sep) {
  StringTokenizer st = new StringTokenizer(s,
→ sep);
  String result[] = new
→ String[st.countTokens()];

  for (int i=0; i<result.length; i++) {
    result[i] = st.nextToken();
  }
  return result;
}


// This method is similar to parse() except that
→ the strings are
// assumed to be decimal integers.  This method
→ coverts these integer
// strings into integers and returns them in an
→ array.
// The result may have zero length but is never
→ null.
int[] parseInt(String s, String sep) {
  StringTokenizer st = new StringTokenizer(s,
→ sep);
  int[] result = new int[st.countTokens()];

  for (int i=0; i<result.length; i++) {
    result[i] = Integer.parseInt(st.nextToken());
  }
  return result;
}

public void paint(Graphics g) {
  imageDone = false;
  update(g);
}

public void update(Graphics g) {
  Graphics g2;

  if (!imageDone) {
    imageDone = g.drawImage(image, 0, 0, this);
    return;
  }

  bbufG.setColor(bgColor);
  bbufG.fillRect(0, 0, size().width, size().
→ height);
  bbufG.drawImage(image, 0, 0, this);

  if (curMenu >= 0) {
    g2 = bbuf.getGraphics();
```

Continued on next page

If we have an URL, we call the getDocumentBase() method using u to get the complete URL.

38. if (getParameter("target") != null) {
    getAppletContext().showDocument(url,
    → getParameter("target"));
}

If the calling HTML file specified a target for the URL, we set it up.

39. else {
    getAppletContext().showDocument(url);
}

Otherwise, we call showDocument() without a target.

40. catch (Exception e) {
    e.printStackTrace();
}

If an exception was triggered, we have a unrecoverable problem, so we just call printStackTrace().

41. public boolean mouseMove(Event evt, int x,
    → int y) {

The mouseMove event is triggered every time the mouse is moved while the cursor is over the menu. This is where a great deal of the applet's most complex work is done.

42. if (curMenu >= 0) {
    int sm = inMenu(menuItemRect, x, y);

If we've been working on a submenu already, we calculate the new cursor location by calling the inMenu() method.

43. if (curMenuItem != sm) {
    curMenuItem = sm;
    repaint();
}

If the location of the cursor has changed the submenu to be highlighted, we reset curMenuItem and repaint the applet.

44. if (sm >= 0) {
    return true;
}
curMenu = -1;

If sm is a number other than -1, it means that the mouse has moved elsewhere in the already-drawn submenu. If this is the case, all that needs to happen is for the highlighting to be redrawn, so we return true. Otherwise, we reinitialize curmenu to -1.

45. int m = inMenu(hitArea, x, y);
    if (m != curMenu) {
        curMenu = m;
        if (m >= 0) {

We use the inMenu() method to calculate the new menu, and if one is found we perform steps 46-55.

46. int maxWidth = 50;
    int maxHeight = 0;
    menuItemRect = new Rectangle[item
    → [curMenu].length];

These lines initialize maxWidth and maxHeight, and declare the new menuItemRect array.

47. for (int i=0; i<menuItemRect.length; i++) {

This tells the applet to do the following for each submenu option.

48. String[] line = parse(item[curMenu][i],
    getParameter("newline"));
    for (int j=0; j<line.length; j++) {

We use the newline value to calculate how many lines this submenu option will take up in the submenu, and then execute the following loop that many times.

49. int w = fm.stringWidth(line[j]);
    if (w > maxWidth) {
        maxWidth = w;
    }

Here we calculate the required width of the submenu based on the text to be displayed.

Applet 14.1 *continued*

```
                         Applet

    // Paint the overlay image
    g2.clipRect(dstPt[curMenu].x, dstPt[curMenu]
  → .y, srcRect[curMenu].width, srcRect
  → [curMenu].height);
    g2.drawImage(image, dstPt[curMenu].x-
  → srcRect[curMenu].x, dstPt[curMenu].y-
  → srcRect[curMenu].y, this);
    g2.dispose();

    g2 = bbuf.getGraphics();
    for (int i=0; i<menuItemRect.length; i++) {
      drawMenuItem(g2, i);
    }
    g2.dispose();
  }
  g.drawImage(bbuf, 0, 0, this);
}

void drawMenuItem(Graphics g, int i) {
  int x, y, w, height;
  // break the menu item label into lines.
  String[] line = parse(item[curMenu][i],
  → getParameter("newline"));

  int hi = 0;
  if (i == curMenuItem) {
    hi = 1;
    getAppletContext().showStatus(itemUrl[curMenu
  → [i]);
  }
  g.setColor(bgMenuColor[hi]);
  g.fillRect(menuItemRect[i].x, menuItemRect
  → [i].y, menuItemRect[i].width, menuItemRect
  → [i].height);

  // set color for text and box
  g.setColor(fgMenuColor[hi]);

  // draw box around menu item.
  g.drawRect(menuItemRect[i].x, menuItemRect
  → [i].y, menuItemRect[i].width, menuItemRect
  → [i].height);

  // draw label
  g.setFont(f);
  y = menuItemRect[i].y + marginV;
  for (i=0; i<line.length; i++) {
    g.drawString(line[i], menuItemRect
  → [i].x+menuItemRect[i].width-fm.stringWidth
  → (line[i])-marginH, y + fm.getAscent());
    y += fm.getHeight();
  }
}

public boolean mouseExit(Event evt, int x,
  → int y) {
  curMenuItem = curMenu = -1;
  repaint();
  return true;
}
```

Continued on next page

Applet 14.1 *continued*

```
                    Applet
public boolean mouseEnter(Event evt, int x,
→ int y) {
  return mouseMove(evt, x, y);
}

public boolean mouseDown(Event evt, int x,
→ int y) {
  try {
    String u = null;

    if (curMenuItem >= 0 && itemUrl[curMenu]
    → .length > 0) {
      u = itemUrl[curMenu][curMenuItem];
    }
    else
      if (curMenu >= 0) {
        u = url[curMenu];
      }
    if (u != null) {
      URL url = new URL (getDocumentBase(), u);

      if (getParameter("target") != null) {
        getAppletContext().showDocument(url, get
        → Parameter("target"));
      }
      else {
        getAppletContext().showDocument(url);
      }
    }
  }
  catch (Exception e) {
    e.printStackTrace();
  }
  return true;
}

public boolean mouseMove(Event evt, int x,
→ int y) {
  if (curMenu >= 0) {
    int sm = inMenu(menuItemRect, x, y);

    if (curMenuItem != sm) {
      curMenuItem = sm;
      repaint();
    }
    if (sm >= 0) {
      return true;
    }
    curMenu = -1;
  }

  int m = inMenu(hitArea, x, y);
  if (m != curMenu) {
    curMenu = m;

    // A new menu is now active so compute
    → menuItemRect.
    if (m >= 0) {
      // Minimum width
      int maxWidth = 50;
      int maxHeight = 0;
```

Continued on next page

50. menuItemRect[i] = new Rectangle();
menuItemRect[i].height = parse(item
→ [curMenu][i], getParameter("newline"))
→ .length * fm.getHeight() + 2 * marginV;
→ maxHeight += menuItemRect[i].height;

Now we calculate the height based on the number of lines, and reset the maxHeight.

51. maxWidth += 2 * marginH + 1;

When the loop has completed, we add the desired horizontal margins to the maxWidth, plus one extra pixel for the left edge.

52. if (down[m]) {
    y = Math.max(0, Math.min(size().height
    → -maxHeight-1, dstPt[curMenu].y +
    → srcRect[curMenu].height-1));
}
else {
    y = Math.max(0, Math.min(size().height
    → -maxHeight-1, dstPt[curMenu].y -
    → maxHeight));
}

A submenu can be displayed either below the chosen menu option or above it. Either way, this code calculates the value of the y-position.

53. x = dstPt[curMenu].x + srcRect[curMenu].
→ width-maxWidth-1;

This calculates the x-position for the display of the submenu.

54. for (int i=0; i<item[curMenu].length; i++) {
    menuItemRect[i].x = x;
    menuItemRect[i].y = y;
    menuItemRect[i].width =
    y += menuItemRect[i].height;
}

For each item in the submenu, we save the x and y positions and the maxWidth, then increment y.

55. getAppletContext().showStatus
→ (url[curMenu]);

We display the URL of the chosen sub-menu option on the browser's status line.

56. int inMenu(Rectangle[] rs, int x, int y) {
    if (rs != null) {
        for (int i=0; i<rs.length;
      → i++) {
          if (rs[i].inside
        → (x, y)) {
            return i;
          }
        }
    }
    return -1;
}

The inMenu() method returns the index of the rectangle in rs containing x and y. If rs is null or x or y is not in rs, it returns -1.

And that's all there is to this nifty applet. Moving the cursor from option to option causes the mouseMove event to be triggered, which then displays the applicable submenu.

Applet 14.1 *continued*

```
                               Applet

 menuItemRect = new Rectangle[item
→[curMenu].length];
 for (int i=0; i<menuItemRect.length; i++) {
   String[] line = parse(item[curMenu][i],
   →getParameter("newline"));

   for (int j=0; j<line.length; j++) {
     int w = fm.stringWidth(line[j]);
     if (w > maxWidth) {
       maxWidth = w;
     }
   }

   menuItemRect[i] = new Rectangle();
   menuItemRect[i].height =
   →parse(item[curMenu][i],
   →getParameter("newline")).
   →length * fm.getHeight() → + 2 * marginV;
   maxHeight += menuItemRect[i].height;
 }

 // Add one extra pixel for the left edge.
 maxWidth += 2 * marginH + 1;
 if (down[m]) {
   y = Math.max(0, Math.min(size().height-
   →maxHeight-1, dstPt[curMenu].y +
   →srcRect[curMenu].height-1)); }
 else {
   y = Math.max(0, Math.min(size().height-
   →maxHeight-1, dstPt[curMenu].y -
   →maxHeight));
 }
 x = dstPt[curMenu].x + srcRect[curMenu].
 →width-maxWidth-1;
 for (int i=0; i<item[curMenu].length; i++) {
   menuItemRect[i].x = x;
   menuItemRect[i].y = y;
   menuItemRect[i].width = maxWidth;
   y += menuItemRect[i].height;
 }
 getAppletContext().showStatus
 →(url[curMenu]);
 }
 repaint();
 }
 return true;
}

// Returns the index of the rectangle in rs
→ containing x and y.
// Returns -1 if either rs is null or x and y is
→ not in rs.
int inMenu(Rectangle[] rs, int x, int y) {
 if (rs != null) {
   for (int i=0; i<rs.length; i++) {
     if (rs[i].inside(x, y)) {
       return i;
     }
   }
 }
 return -1;
}
}
```

Table 14.1

Applet Parameters

PARAMETER	DESCRIPTION	EXAMPLE
bg-color	Specifies a color to paint behind the background image. This color is only visible if the background image has transparent pixels or if the applet is larger than the background image.	
bg-hi-menu-color	The color to paint the background of highlighted menu items. The color is specified by an RGB triplet of three decimal numbers in the range 0-255.	`<param name=bg-hi-menu-color value="10 10 10">`
bg-menu-color	The color to paint the background of the menu items. The color is specified by an RGB triplet of three decimal numbers in the range 0-255.	`<param name=bg-menu-color value="0 255 0">`
fg-hi-menu-color	The color to paint the text of highlighted menu item labels. The color is specified by an RGB triplet of three decimal numbers in the range 0-255.	`<param name=fg-hi-menu-color value="255 255 255">`
fg-menu-color	The color to paint the text of the menu item labels. The color is specified by an RGB triplet of three decimal numbers in the range 0-255.	`<param name=fg-menu-color value="0 0 0">`
font	The font type to use for the menu items. There are only three possible values: Helvetica, TimesRoman, and Courier.	`<param name=font value="Helvetica">`
font-height	The pixel height of the font to use for the menu items.	`<param name=font-height value="14">`
image	Names the file containing the background image and the rollover images.	`<param name=image value="background.gif">`
marginh	The number of pixels to the left and right of the menu item labels.	`<param name=marginh value="2">`
marginv	The number of pixels above and below each menu item label.	`<param name=marginv value="2">`
menuX	X starts at 0 and increases upwards by 1. The value of this parameter is made up of five non-optional values, separated by the separator character described above. There may also be a pair of optional values that specify the menu items for the menu. If no values are specified, no menu will appear when the cursor moves into the hotbox. These pairs are repeated for each menu label. See Figure 14.2 for the values of the fields.	`<param name=menu0 value="0 0 148 18	148 0 148 18	0 0	d	/nav/whatis/index.html	Intro FAQ	/nav/whatis/introfaq.html	Java Story	/nav/whatis/index.html">`
newline	Specifies the character used to force a newline in a menu item.	`<param name=separator value="^">`
separator	Specifies the character used to separate items in menuX parameters.	`<param name=separator value="|">`
target	If present, specifies the target frame that will show the new URL.	`<param name=target value="otherframe">`

WHERE TO LEARN MORE

While every author dreams that their book is everything that anyone would want to know about the subject, the truth is that Java is too complex a topic to cover completely in a book of this size and style. If what you've learned so far has you interested in learning more about Java, here are some resources to get you started.

Java on the Web

As would be expected with a language that started on the Web, there are numerous Web pages devoted to Java. Here are some sites that I've found to be worth seeing.

Sun's Java site

http://java.sun.com or
http://www.javasoft.com

This is Sun's home for Java on the Web (Figure A.1). Because Sun developed Java, this is always the place to start for the latest and greatest information. When you want documentation on, for example, Java APIs, you know that here you're getting the word straight from the horse's mouth.

Gamelan: The Official Directory for Java

http://www.developer.com/directories/pages/
→ dir.java.html or
http://www.gamelan.com

As described earlier, Gamelan is the repository of many of the best applets on the Web (Figure A.2). This is where to start when you're looking for other people's applets to use on your pages (after getting their permission, of course!). Gamelan's categories include Arts and Entertainment, Business and Finance, Commercial Java, Educational, Games, How-To, JavaBeans, Multimedia, Network and Communications, Programming in Java, Publications, Sites, Special Effects, and Tools and Utilities.

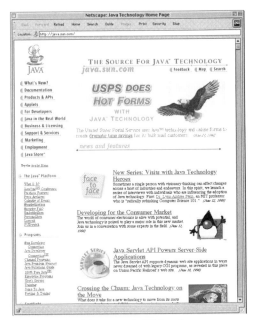

Figure A.1 Java's home on the Web, at Sun

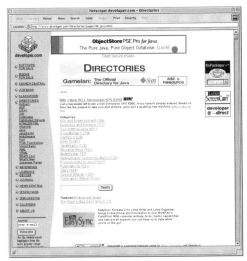

Figure A.2 The Gamelan Directory is one of the best sites for applets on the Web.

Figure A.3 JARS will rate your efforts and give you a snazzy badge to put on your site if you qualify.

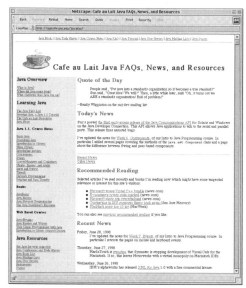

Figure A.4 Café au Lait—Java FAQs, news, and resources

The Java Review Service (JARS)

http://www.jars.com

If, after reading this book, you write an applet that is just so new and wonderful you want the world to know about it, submit your page to JARS for evaluation (Figure A.3). Applets are judged on quality and innovation. If you make the grade, you'll get a link from their site to yours, and a badge you can display to show that you are now a Java wiz.

Then again, if you're still looking for examples to help you make your applets sing and dance, you can also check out other people's code here to see exactly how the wizards did it.

Café au Lait

http://sunsite.unc.edu/javafaq/

Every technology needs a FAQ (frequently asked questions) page; Java's is Café au Lait (Figure A.4). While a little outdated (as of this writing), this site, maintained by author Elliotte Rusty Harold, still includes a great list of Java news and resources.

Online magazines

Early in Java's development, several magazine companies tried to start up publications to serve the Java community. Most of them later fell victim to "Web time"—in the lag between the articles being completed and the magazine arriving in the readers' hands, weeks had passed, and Web-savvy Java developers had long since read the news online. While a few publications are still selling print subscriptions, all of the following also have active Web sites.

Javaworld Magazine

http://www.javaworld.com

The last survivor of the big-time publishers' attempts at Java magazines, this is now an online-only publication from IDG (Figure A.5). Monthly and bimonthly columns include Java In Depth, Java Step by Step, JavaBeans, How-To Java, Design Techniques, Java Developer, Distributed Objects, Media Programming, and Java Tips.

Java Report

http://www.javareport.com

A subscription to the print edition is $39 per year for individuals in the USA, but the online version has most of the same content.

Java Developer's Journal

http://www.JavaDevelopersJournal.com

An annual subscription to the Java Developer's Journal is $39.99, but you can sign up at the Web site to get a free trial issue (Figure A.6). The complete digital edition requires a subscription, but many features are public.

Java Pro

http://www.java-pro.com

Java Pro is another print magazine with its content available online.

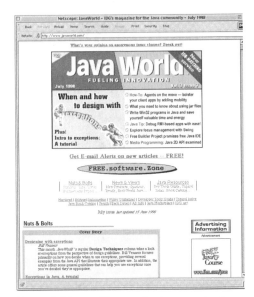

Figure A.5 Javaworld—an online Java magazine from IDG

Figure A.6 The Java Developer's Journal in its online form

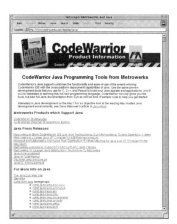

Figure A.7 CodeWarrior Pro is a great choice if you program in multiple languages on multiple platforms.

Figure A.8 IBM's VisualAge for Java was highly rated by Javaworld magazine.

Figure A.9 Borland JBuilder 2 is now a product of Inprise.

Integrated Development Environments (IDEs)

For most languages they're called compilers, but Java isn't most languages. To do serious Java development, you're going to need a development environment. Here are the major players (in no particular order).

Metrowerks' CodeWarrior Pro

http://www.metrowerks.com/desktop/java/

Along with a Java IDE, this package includes compilers for C, C++, and Pascal (Figure A.7). You can download CodeWarrior Lite from the site for free to check it out before you buy the complete package. For Windows 95/NT and Macintosh.

Sun Microsystems' Java Workshop 2.0

http://www.sun.com/software/Developer-
→ products/java

This is the IDE from the folks who brought you Java. For Windows 95/NT, Solaris, HP-UX, and Unixware.

IBM's VisualAge for Java

http://www.software.ibm.com/ad/vajava

A recent Javaworld roundup labeled this as the best of the Windows visual Java tools (Figure A.8). For Windows 95/NT and OS/2.

Inprise's Borland JBuilder 2

http://www.inprise.com/jbuilder

While Borland has changed its name to Inprise, it's still been making good development tools for many years, including the Java IDE Jbuilder 2 (Figure A.9). For Windows 95/NT.

INTEGRATED DEVELOPMENT ENVIRONMENTS (IDEs)

Microsoft's Visual J++ 6.0

http://www.microsoft.com/visualj

Well, Sun won't let Microsoft call it Java, so they're calling this package J++ to make it sound like C++ (Figure A.10). No matter what you call it, it's the MS-ized version of Java. This site includes links to resources such as developer programs and technical materials. For (surprise!) Windows 95/NT.

SuperCede 2.0 Professional

http://www.supercede.com

SuperCede was formed as a spinoff of Asymetrix, and the SuperCede for Java Standard Edition is a free download. For Windows 95/NT.

Symantec's Visual Café

http://www.symantec.com/domain/cafe/vc4java. → html

Visual Café is a good visual tool for cross-platform Java development (Figure A.11). A database edition is available, providing easy connectivity for your Java apps. For Windows 95/NT and Macintosh.

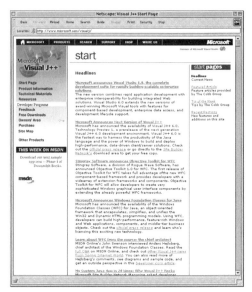

Figure A.10 Sun won't let them call it Java, so Microsoft calls it J++.

Figure A.11 Symantec's Visual Café is a cross-platform visual development tool.

Java books

The book you're looking at now is just an introductory text—there's a lot more to this language! Here are a few of the best books to check out of you want to take the next step.

Java in a Nutshell

Everything you always wanted to know about Java but didn't even know where to ask is in this book. Written by David Flanagan and published by O'Reilly and Associates, *Java in a Nutshell* is a great reference.

Java Examples in a Nutshell

This book is a companion guide to the previous volume, and is again written by David Flanagan and published by O'Reilly and Associates. While *Java in a Nutshell* is an excellent reference, it has virtually no examples. This book makes up for that lack, though the examples given assume a programming background.

Graphic Java: Mastering the AWT

This SunSoft Press book by David M. Geary tells you everything you need to know about the AWT, including an in-depth look at each of the layout managers. If you're working with the AWT, you'll eventually need this book.

Just Java and Beyond 1.1

This is another SunSoft Press book, this time by Peter van der Linden. I'm not recommending this book because it's a good way to learn more about Java (although it is) or because the author knows his material inside and out (although he does), I recommend it because the index includes the following entry: "Recursion joke, old: see Recursion joke, old." The book (in my older edition) also contains references to Mr. Potato Head, rhino farts, and goobers. In other words, if you like excellent writing about Java mixed with a really wacky sense of humor, this may be for you, too.

Newsgroups

In the far distant past, there was one comp.lang.java newsgroup, and virtually overnight it became extremely busy. Consequently, it was split up into many little Java newsgroups, most of which are carried by major news servers.

The following is a list of the newsgroups that my server carries (see Figure A.12). Your news server may not carry all of these, but it may also carry some that aren't here.

- comp.lang.java
- comp.lang.java.advocacy
- comp.lang.java.announce
- comp.lang.java.api
- comp.lang.java.databases
- comp.lang.java.developer
- comp.lang.java.gui
- comp.lang.java.help
- comp.lang.java.machine
- comp.lang.java.misc
- comp.lang.java.programmer
- comp.lang.java.security
- comp.lang.java.setup
- comp.lang.java.softwaretools
- comp.lang.java.tech

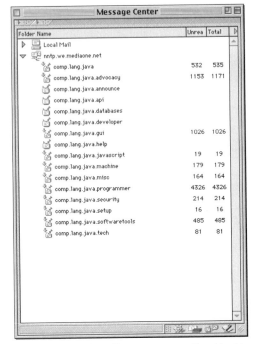

Figure A.12 The list of Java newsgroups offered by this news server

✔ Tip

■ Usenet is not a friendly place for people who are considered to be "newbies." Asking what old-timers consider to be a stupid question can bring nasty messages in response ("flaming"). At a minimum, always read a couple of days' worth of messages before posting your first message, and always read the FAQ!

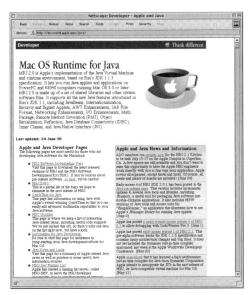

Figure A.13 Apple's home for Java development on the Mac

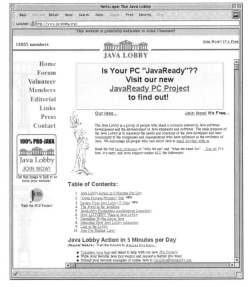

Figure A.14 Who's suing whom this week? The Java Lobby sure knows who they think is in the right or in the wrong.

Cross-platform Issues

The original promise of Java was "write once, run anywhere." Here are two sites that have little in common except a strong commitment to that philosophy.

Apple Java Developer pages

http://devworld.apple.com/java

If you're developing Java applets or applications where you want Mac compatibility, you need to check out this site (Figure A.13). While Sun handles Java for UNIX systems, and both Sun and Microsoft try to handle Java for Wintel systems, Apple has the sole responsibility for updating Java on the Mac. Consequently, it always seems to be a little behind and a little slow. However, you should at least try out your programs on the Mac to be absolutely sure that you've handled all the cross-platform issues. This site includes links to the MRJ (Macintosh Runtime for Java) bug list and the MRJ-Dev e-mail list.

The Java Lobby

http://www.javalobby.org

These are the folks fighting the good fight for an open and standard Java (Figure A.14). For them, 99% pure Java just isn't quite good enough. This is an excellent resource site for finding out what all the fuss and lawsuits are about.

RESERVED WORDS

Reserved words are those words that have special meanings to a programming language. Therefore, they may not be used as names for variables, classes, or methods.

Most of the following words should be familiar from earlier parts of the book, though some are either outside the scope of this book or are words being reserved in anticipation of future usage.

Java's reserved words

These words are reserved by Java. While it's true that they are all lowercase and that Java, being case-sensitive, will allow you to name (for instance) a variable with a mixed-case version of any of these words, it's considered to be very bad programming style. At the least, it will make your code hard to understand and maintain.

abstract

Declares that a class cannot be instantiated.

boolean

A data type that can only be either true or false.

byte

An 8-bit single-character data type.

case

Used in a switch statement to execute one of several sections of code depending on the value of a variable.

catch

Used to trap errors within a try block.

char

A 16-bit single-character data type.

class

A hierarchical collection of data and methods that act upon that data.

continue

Skips all following statements in a loop and continues with the next iteration of the loop.

default

Executes statements in a switch block if all cases within the switch block are false.

do

Used with a "while" to loop.

double

A double-precision floating point number.

else

Used within an if statement structure to execute a block of statements when whatever the if statement tests for evaluates to false.

extends

When one class extends another class, it inherits from that class.

false

A constant, which is always set to false.

final

When a class is declared final it cannot be inherited. When a method is declared final it cannot be overridden. Declaring a variable final makes it a non-modifiable constant.

finally

Forces a block of code to always be executed in a try...catch block.

float

A single-precision floating point number.

for

A loop with initialization, condition testing, and a statement to be run during each iteration.

if

Tests a condition and then executes a block of code when that condition is true.

implements

Defines a class as using an interface.

import

Makes Java classes available to the current class under an abbreviated name.

instanceof

Tests whether a variable is an instance of a particular class or implements a particular interface.

int

An integer number.

interface

Contains methods that are grouped together. Classes implement interfaces to use their methods.

long

A very large integer number.

native

Declares a function as external to Java. The method is implemented in a platform-dependent language such as C or C++.

new

Creates a new instance of an object, including allocating memory and initializing variables.

null

All instances of classes are initialized to null (a constant) until set up with a new command or assigned to an existing class.

package

A group of classes bundled together.

private

Only visible to the class that defined it.

protected

Only visible within the package that defined it.

public

Visible anywhere its class or package is visible.

return

Sends control (and sometimes variables) back from a method to its calling method.

short

A small integer number.

static

Static methods have one and only one instance per class, invoked through the class name.

super

Accesses ancestor attributes that were overridden by descendant attributes.

switch

Executes one of several code blocks depending on the value of a variable.

synchronized

Only one thread is allowed to run in this method at a time.

this

Refers to the current instance of a class.

throw

Forces an error to occur.

throws

Indicates that this method can cause the thrown exception or error.

transient

A scratch variable for a class, which is neither saved with a class nor cloned to other instances of a class.

true

A constant, which is always set to true.

try

Sets up an error-catching block in which any errors caught are processed by catch and finally by code blocks.

void

This method does not return a value to its calling method.

volatile

This variable may be changed at any time, so no code optimization should be allowed.

while

Used with the do statement to perform a loop.

Words reserved but not yet used in Java

The following words have been reserved by Java, though they are not yet in use.

byvalue	inner
cast	operator
const	outer
future	rest
generic	var
goto	

Reserved method names

The following method names are reserved.

clone	notify
equals	notifyAll
finalize	toString
getClass	wait
hashCode	

Reserved characters

The following characters may not be used in variable names. Doing so will cause Java to try to evaluate the variables as statements, and you'll just end up with a mess on your hands.

+	*	(	;
-	|	)	?
!	-	{	,
%	/	}	.
^	<	[	
&	>	]	

THE JAVA OBJECT HIERARCHY

As Java is an object-oriented language, its classes fall into a strict object hierarchy. This appendix lays out the classes and interfaces for each of the major Java packages.

In each of the following tables, objects in italics were introduced in JDK 1.1.

The java.applet Package

Table C.1

java.applet Classes and Interfaces

CLASS	ABSTRACT CLASS	INTERFACE	EXCEPTION
Applet	–	AppletContext	–
–	–	AppletStub	–
–	–	AudioClip	–

The java.awt Package

Table C.2

java.awt Classes and Interfaces

CLASS	ABSTRACT CLASS	INTERFACE	EXCEPTION
AWTError	*AWTEvent*	*Adjustable*	AWTException
AWTEventMulticaster	Graphics	*ItemSelectable*	*IllegalComponentStateException*
BorderLayout	Component	LayoutManager	–
Button	Container	*LayoutManager2*	–
Canvas	FontMetrics	MenuContainer	–
CardLayout	Image	*PrintGraphics*	–
Checkbox	*PrintJob*	*Shape*	–
CheckboxGroup	MenuComponent	–	–
CheckboxMenuItem	Toolkit	–	–
Choice	–	–	–
Color	–	–	–
Cursor	–	–	–
Dialog	–	–	–
Dimension	–	–	–
Event	–	–	–
EventQueue	–	–	–
FileDialog	–	–	–
FlowLayout	–	–	–
Font	–	–	–
Frame	–	–	–
GridBagConstraints	–	–	–
GridBagLayout	–	–	–

Table C.2 continued

java.awt Classes and Interfaces

CLASS	ABSTRACT CLASS	INTERFACE	EXCEPTION
GridLayout	–	–	–
Insets	–	–	–
Label	–	–	–
List	–	–	–
MediaTracker	–	–	–
Menu	–	–	–
MenuBar	–	–	–
MenuItem	–	–	–
MenuShortcut	–	–	–
Panel	–	–	–
Point	–	–	–
Polygon	–	–	–
PopupMenu	–	–	–
Rectangle	–	–	–
Scrollbar	–	–	–
ScrollPane	–	–	–
SystemColor	–	–	–
TextArea	–	–	–
TextComponent	–	–	–
TextField	–	–	–
Window	–	–	–

The java.awt.datatransfer Package (Introduced in JDK 1.1)

Table C.3

java.awt.datatransfer Classes and Interfaces

CLASS	ABSTRACT CLASS	INTERFACE	EXCEPTION
Clipboard	ClipboardOwner	Transferable	UnsupportedFlavorException
DataFlavor	–	–	–
StringSelection	–	–	–

The java.awt.event Package (Introduced in JDK 1.1)

Table C.4

java.awt.event Classes and Interfaces

CLASS	ABSTRACT CLASS	INTERFACE	EXCEPTION
ActionEvent	ComponentAdaptor	ActionListener	–
AdjustmentEvent	ContainerAdaptor	AdjustmentListener	–
ComponentEvent	FocusAdaptor	ComponentListener	–
ContainerEvent	InputEvent	ContainerListener	–
FocusEvent	KeyAdaptor	FocusListener	–
ItemEvent	MouseAdaptor	ItemListener	–
KeyEvent	MouseMotionAdaptor	KeyListener	–
MouseEvent	WindowAdaptor	MouseListener	–
PaintEvent	–	MouseMotionListener	–
TextEvent	–	TextListener	–
WindowEvent	–	WindowListener	–

The java.awt.image Package

Table C.5

java.awt.image Classes and Interfaces

CLASS	ABSTRACT CLASS	INTERFACE	EXCEPTION
AreaAveragingScaleFilter	ColorModel	ImageConsumer	–
CropImageFilter	RGBImageFilter	ImageObserver	–
DirectColorModel	–	ImageProducer	–
FilteredImageSource	–	–	–
ImageFilter	–	–	–
IndexColorModel	–	–	–
MemoryImageSource	–	–	–
PixelGrabber	–	–	–
ReplicateScaleFilter	–	–	–

The java.awt.peer Package

Table C.6

java.awt.peer Classes and Interfaces

CLASS	ABSTRACT CLASS	INTERFACE	EXCEPTION
–	–	ButtonPeer	–
–	–	CanvasPeer	–
–	–	CheckboxMenuItemPeer	–
–	–	CheckboxPeer	–
–	–	ChoicePeer	–
–	–	ComponentPeer	–
–	–	ContainerPeer	–
–	–	DialogPeer	–
–	–	FileDialogPeer	–
–	–	*FontPeer*	–
–	–	FramePeer	–
–	–	LabelPeer	–
–	–	*LightweightPeer*	–
–	–	ListPeer	–
–	–	MenuBarPeer	–
–	–	MenuComponentPeer	–
–	–	MenuItemPeer	–
–	–	MenuPeer	–
–	–	PanelPeer	–
–	–	*PopupMenuPeer*	–
–	–	*ScrollPanelPeer*	–
–	–	ScrollbarPeer	–
–	–	TextAreaPeer	–
–	–	TextComponentPeer	–
–	–	TextFieldPeer	–
–	–	WindowPeer	–

The java.beans Package (Introduced in JDK 1.1)

Table C.7

java.beans Classes and Interfaces

CLASS	ABSTRACT CLASS	INTERFACE	EXCEPTION
BeanDescriptor	–	BeanInfo	IntrospectionException
Beans	–	Customizer	PropertyVetoException
EventSetDescriptor	–	PropertyChangeListener	–
FeatureDescriptor	–	PropertyEditor	–
IndexedPropertyDescriptor	–	VetoableChangeListener	–
Introspector	–	Visibility	–
IntrospectorMethodDescriptor	–	–	–
ParameterDescriptor	–	–	–
PropertyChangeEvent	–	–	–
PropertyChangeSupport	–	–	–
PropertyDescriptor	–	–	–
PropertyEditorManager	–	–	–
PropertyEditorSupport	–	–	–
SimpleBeanInfo	–	–	–
VetoableChangeSupport	–	–	–

The java.io Package

Table C.8

java.io Classes and Interfaces

CLASS	ABSTRACT CLASS	INTERFACE	EXCEPTION
BufferedInputStream	Externizable	DataInput	CharConversionException
BufferedOutputStream	FilterReader	DataOutput	EOFException
BufferedWriter	FilterWriter	FilenameFilter	FileNotFoundException
ByteArrayInputStream	InputStream	ObjectInput	InterruptedIOException
ByteArrayOutputStream	OutputStream	ObjectInputValidation	IOException
CharArrayReader	Reader	ObjectOutput	InvalidClassException
CharArrayWriter	Writer	Serializable	InvalidObjectException
DataInputStream	–	–	NotActiveException
DataOutputStream	–	–	NotSerializableException
File	–	–	ObjectStreamException
FileDescriptor	–	–	OptionalDataException
FileInputStream	–	–	StreamCorruptedException
FileOutputStream	–	–	SyncFailedException
FileReader	–	–	UnsupportedEncodingException
FileWriter	–	–	UTFDataFormatException
FilterInputStream	–	–	WriteAbortedException
FilterOutputStream	–	–	–
InputStreamReader	–	–	–
LineNumberInputStream	–	–	–
LineNumberReader	–	–	–
ObjectInputStream	–	–	–
ObjectOutputStream	–	–	–
ObjectStreamClass	–	–	–
OutputStreamWriter	–	–	–
PipedInputStream	–	–	–
PipedOutputStream	–	–	–
PipedReader	–	–	–
PipedWriter	–	–	–
PrintStream	–	–	–
PrintWriter	–	–	–
PushbackInputStream	–	–	–

Table C.8 continued

java.io Classes and Interfaces

CLASS	ABSTRACT CLASS	INTERFACE	EXCEPTION
PushbackReader	–	–	–
RandomAccessFile	–	–	–
SequenceInputStream	–	–	–
StreamTokenizer	–	–	–
StringBufferInputStream	–	–	–
StringReader	–	–	–
StringWriter	–	–	–

THE JAVA OBJECT HIERARCHY

The java.lang Package

Table C.9
java.lang Classes and Interfaces

CLASS	ABSTRACT CLASS	INTERFACE	EXCEPTION
Boolean	ClassLoader	Cloneable	AbstractMethodError
Byte	–	–	ArithmeticException
Character	Number	–	ArrayIndexOutOfBoundsException
Class	Process	Runnable	ArrayStoreException
Compiler	SecurityManager	–	ClassCastException
Double	VirtualMachineError	–	ClassCircularityError
Float	–	–	ClassFormatError
Integer	–	–	ClassNotFoundException
Long	–	–	CloneNotSupportedException
Math	–	–	Error
Object	–	–	Exception
Runtime	–	–	ExceptionInInitializorError
Short	–	–	IllegalAccessError
String	–	–	IllegalAccessException
StringBuffer	–	–	IllegalArgumentException
System	–	–	IllegalMonitorStateException
Thread	–	–	IllegalStateException
ThreadGroup	–	–	IllegalThreadStateException
Throwable	–	–	IncompatibleClassChangeError
Void	–	–	IndexOutOfBoundsException
–	–	–	InstantiationError
–	–	–	InstantiationException
–	–	–	InternalError
–	–	–	InterruptedException
–	–	–	LinkageError
–	–	–	NoClassDefFoundError
–	–	–	NoSuchFieldError
–	–	–	NoSuchFieldException
–	–	–	NoSuchMethodError
–	–	–	NoSuchMethodException
–	–	–	NullPointerException

Table C.9 continued
java.lang Classes and Interfaces

CLASS	ABSTRACT CLASS	INTERFACE	EXCEPTION
–	–	–	NumberFormatException
–	–	–	OutOfMemoryError
–	–	–	RuntimeException
–	–	–	SecurityException
–	–	–	StackOverflowError
–	–	–	StringIndexOutOfBoundsException
–	–	–	ThreadDeath
–	–	–	UnknownError
–	–	–	UnsatisfiedLinkError
–	–	–	VerifyError

The java.lang.reflect Package (Introduced in JDK 1.1)

Table C.10
java.lang.reflect Classes and Interfaces

CLASS	ABSTRACT CLASS	INTERFACE	EXCEPTION
Array	–	Member	InvocationTargetException
Constructor	–	–	–
Field	–	–	–
Method	–	–	–
Modifier	–	–	–

The java.math Package (Introduced in JDK 1.1)

Table C.11
java.math Classes and Interfaces

CLASS	ABSTRACT CLASS	INTERFACE	EXCEPTION
BigDecimal	–	–	–
BigInteger	–	–	–

The java.net Package

Table C.12
java.net Classes and Interfaces

CLASS	ABSTRACT CLASS	INTERFACE	EXCEPTION
DatagramPacket	ContentHandler	ContentHandlerFactory	*BindException*
DatagramSocket	*DatagramSocketImpl*	*FileNameMap*	*ConnectException*
InetAddress	*HttpURLConnection*	SocketImplFactory	MalformedURLException
MulticastSocket	SocketImpl	URLStreamHandlerFactory	*NoRouteToHostException*
ServerSocket	URLConnection	–	ProtocolException
Socket	URLStreamHandler	–	SocketException
URL	–	–	UnknownHostException
URLEncoder	–	–	UnknownServiceException

The java.text Package (Introduced in JDK 1.1)

Table C.13
java.text Classes and Interfaces

CLASS	ABSTRACT CLASS	INTERFACE	EXCEPTION
ChoiceFormat	BreakIterator	–	ParseException
CollationElementIterator	Collator	CharacterIterator	–
CollationKey	DateFormat	–	–
DateFormatSymbols	Format	–	–
DecimalFormat	NumberFormat	–	–
DecimalFormatSymbols	–	–	–
FieldPosition	–	–	–
MessageFormat	–	–	–
ParsePosition	–	–	–
RuleBasedCollator	–	–	–
SimpleDateFormat	–	–	–
StringCharacterIterator	–	–	–

The java.util Package

Table C.14
java.util Classes and Interfaces

CLASS	ABSTRACT CLASS	INTERFACE	EXCEPTION
BitSet	Dictionary	Enumeration	EmptyStackException
Date	Calendar	EventListener	MissingResourceException
EventObject	ResourceBundle	–	Observer NoSuchElementException
GregorianCalendar	TimeZone	–	TooManyListeners
Hashtable	–	–	–
ListResourceBundle	–	–	–
Locale	–	–	–
Observable	–	–	–
Properties	–	–	–
PropertyResourceBundle	–	–	–
Random	–	–	–
SimpleTimeZone	–	–	–
Stack	–	–	–
StringTokenizer	–	–	–
Vector	–	–	–

THE JAVA OBJECT HIERARCHY

The java.util.zip Package (Introduced in JDK 1.1)

Table C.15

java.util.zip Classes and Interfaces

CLASS	ABSTRACT CLASS	INTERFACE	EXCEPTION
Adler32	–	Checksum	DataFormatException
CheckedInputStream	–	–	ZipException
CheckedOutputStream	–	–	–
CRC32	–	–	–
Deflator	–	–	–
DeflatorOutputStream	–	–	–
GZIPInputStream	–	–	–
GZIPOutputStream	–	–	–
Inflater	–	–	–
InflaterInputStream	–	–	–
ZipEntry	–	–	–
ZipFile	–	–	–
ZipInputStream	–	–	–
ZipOutputStream	–	–	–

DIFFERENCES BETWEEN JDKS 1.0 AND 1.1

Whenever a programming language is changed, programmers are forced to adapt. Not all the changes to the Java language concern the typical applet programmer; this appendix should help you to understand the relevant changes.

The most significant change is to the Java Event Model, the way that you make an applet respond to the user. This will be the hardest new thing to learn, as it changes the structure of the program itself. The other changes give you new capabilities, so you won't have to make any changes to your code unless you want to. The main thing to remember is that these changes were made to help make programming easier, not to give you headaches. The new Event Model was created to establish consistency and so that Java could be more easily used with programming tools.

You might wonder why the old Event Model is still taught, especially if the new one is so good. The reason is that if you're writing for the Web, the majority of the people on the Net still don't have a Web browser that is capable of using Java 1.1. Until that changes, it is best to design applets that can reach the maximum number of people by using 1.0.

The New Event Model

In the model you have been using up to this point, events were handled using the Event class. In order to have your applet respond to user clicking on a button, for example, you would write a method called action, and then use the Event object that was passed in to determine specifically whether a button was pressed.

This model seems pretty straightforward, and it is for very small applets. However, as your programs grow larger it becomes very hard to determine which events belong to which components. This model is also bad for performance, as the system has to check every event that happens whether it is relevant or not.

The new model seems a bit more complex, but once you master it it makes everything even easier, particularly when you have more than one class cooperating on a page. The concept is that for every event, you have a listener. The listener is registered with the source of the event. The listener will have the methods that are appropriate for that type of event, and those methods are called just as they are in the old Event Model.

For example, if you want to respond to a button press, you have to make your applet into an *ActionListener*. The applet is then registered to listen to the button with a new method called addActionListener(). In the example below, I used the keyword this to register the applet as an ActionListener for the button. Any object (including applets) can become an ActionListener by implementing the ActionListener interface, which specifies that the object has to have a method called actionPerformed. This method will be called when the button is pressed, just as the action() method was called in the old Event Model.

Handling a button press with JDK 1.0

```
public class ButtonApplet extends Applet{

Button b;

public void init(){
   b=new Button("Press Me");
   add(b);
}

public boolean action(Event e, Object arg){
   if(e.target instanceof Button)...here is
   → where you would put the code to react
   → to the button press...
```

Handling a button press with JDK 1.1

```
public class ButtonApplet extends Applet
implements ActionListener{

Button b;

public void init(){
   b=new Button("press me");
   b.addActionListener(this);
   add(b);
}

public void actionPerformed(ActionEvent e){
   if(e.getSource() instanceof Button){
   ...here is where you would put the code to
   → react to a button press...
```

Table D.1

Events in Java 1.1		
INTERFACE	**COMPONENTS**	**METHODS**
ActionListener	Button List MenuItem TextField	actionPerformed()
AdjustmentListener	Scrollbar	adjustmentValueChanged()
ComponentListener	All components	componentHidden() componentMoved() componentResized() componentShown()
ContainerListener	All containers	componentAdded() componentRemoved()
FocusListener	All components	focusGained() focusLost()
ItemListener	Checkbox CheckboxMenuItem Choice List	itemStateChanged()
KeyListener	All components	keyPressed() keyReleased() keyTyped()
MouseListener	All components	mouseClicked() mouseEntered() mouseExited() mousePressed() mouseReleased()
MouseMotionListener	All components	mouseDragged() mouseMoved()
TextListener	TextComponent	textValueChanged()
WindowListener	Window	windowActivated() windowClosed() windowClosing() windowDeactivated() windowDeiconified() windowIconified() windowOpened()

It might seem strange that you have to register the applet with the button when the first example did not need to do anything to find the right method. The reason behind the change is that it aids performance. The old Event Model forces the machine to check every object for an action() method every time something happens. That means that the system is being tied up every time a key is pressed or a mouse is moved, regardless of whether or not the program really cares about those events. With this model, the applet only responds to the events that really matter.

The other events are handled in the same way as button presses. Each event has its own interface, which in turn has a set of methods that must be implemented. Table D.1 shows the different kinds of event listeners, the components that generate those types of events, and the methods that are used in the interface to respond to the events.

Although the new Event Model seems a little more complicated, it is actually much easier to use when you are trying to have several objects respond to a single event source.

The main complication with using either of the Event Models, old or new, is that you have to write that pesky if statement to determine which event you are handling. It is not uncommon for an applet to have more than one button, or a button and a list. This means that you have to determine which component was the source of the event, which can lead to long, overly complex methods. This problem was addressed in JDK 1.1 with the introduction of inner classes.

Inner Classes

The new Event Model would be overly cumbersome if not for the introduction of inner classes. This change to Java's syntax allows you to define one class inside of another. This is very useful for people who write

THE NEW EVENT MODEL

complicated programs that need very specialized objects, but it also has a use that you can apply right now. There is a particular kind of inner class, called an *anonymous inner class.*, which is useful for applet programmers. The anonymous inner class takes the complexity out of the Event Model.

Here is the same example as before, but this time using an anonymous inner class. Just to show how much easier event handling is using this technique, there are two buttons instead of just one.

As you can see, there is no longer any need for complicated decision logic to determine which button was pressed. The inner class allows you to define the event handling at the button itself, rather than at one central location. There is no longer any need to find out whether the source of the event was a button, and more importantly, there is no need to determine which button was pressed if there was more than one.

Method Names

Many of the methods that already existed in JDK 1.0 have been renamed in JDK 1.1. Although it is hard to see why this kind of change would be necessary, the new method names are more consistent. This makes programming easier, but it was really done so that Java could be manipulated by advanced programming tools. The term that is used in the Java documentation to mark a method as out-of-date is "deprecated."

There are two large categories of methods called accessors and mutators. *Accessors* are methods that return the value of some variable. *Mutators* are methods that change the value of a variable. The accessors in JDK 1.1 use the word "get" with the name of the variable appended, while the mutators use the word "set" with the name of the variable appended, as shown by the examples in Table D.2.

Handling a button press with an anonymous inner class

```
public class ButtonApplet extends  Applet
implements ActionListener{

Button b, c;

public void init(){
    b=new Button("press me");
    b.addActionListener(new  ActionListener(){
        public void actionPerformed
      → (ActionEvent e){
            ...do stuff here...
        }
    }
    c=new Button("press me, too");
    c.addActionListener(new ActionListener(){
        public void actionPerformed
      → (ActionEvent e){
            ...do stuff for button c...
        }
    }
    add(b);
    add(c);
}
```

Table D.2

Comparison of Method Names in JDK 1.0 and JDK 1.1	
JDK 1.0 METHOD NAME	JDK 1.1 METHOD NAME
size()	getSize()
resize()	setSize()
location()	getLocation()
move()	setLocation()
enable(), disable()	setEnable()

These changed methods are found throughout the AWT, so it is a good thing to be aware of if you are switching to JDK 1.1. There is a more comprehensive guide on the Web at the following address: http://java.sun.com/docs/books/tutorial/
→ post1.0/converting/deprecatedAWT.html.

Jar Files

Jar stands for "Java archive." You can use jar files to package many Java class files or other resource files (graphics or sounds, for example) into one big file, with the extension ".jar" on the end. Most current browsers support jar files, and you will learn how to put them into Web pages in the next section. There are several reasons to use jar files:

◆ Files that are packaged together transfer more quickly over the Net.

◆ It is easier to manage and track one big file than many small files.

◆ If files are grouped together, they can be manipulated as one unit (this is necessary for digital signatures).

The ‹APPLET› Tag

There are two new attributes for the APPLET tag in JDK 1.1. The ARCHIVE attribute allows you to specify a jar file (or a list of jar files) for the browser to download. When you use this attribute, the rest of your <APPLET> tag will probably look pretty much the same, for example:

```
<APPLET ARCHIVE="myJarName.jar"
→ CODE="appletName.class" HEIGHT=100
→ WIDTH=200></APPLET>
```

There is also another new attribute called OBJECT. You will probably not use this much unless you get into advanced Java programming. The OBJECT attribute is used in conjunction with a technique called serialization. *Serialization* is used to store an object

THE NEW EVENT MODEL

so that it can continue being used at a later time. An example is when you are playing a video game and you want to save your game to continue later. If you want to embed a serialized applet into a Web page, you would replace the CODE attribute with OBJECT:

```
<APPLET OBJECT="mySerializedApplet.ser"
→ HEIGHT=320 WIDTH=240></APPLET>
```

Other Changes

There have been a number of other changes to the JDK, far too many to even mention in this appendix. However, some of these things might become useful to you as you continue to explore Java programming. There is also another upgrade in the works, JDK 1.2, which is still in beta at the time of this writing.

There is a new applet method in Java 1.1 called getLocale(). This method is used with a new feature called internationalization, which allows you to embed location-specific information into your applet. Whenever someone runs the applet, their computer will automatically run the applet using the correct information for that locale. If all of the strings in an applet are internationalized, the applet will be accessible to Web viewers all over the world, not just in the country of origin.

Another feature that you might find handy is the digital signature. This allows you to get out of the so-called "sandbox" that was discussed earlier in this book. When an applet is digitally signed, the user can be absolutely sure who wrote the applet, and that it hasn't been modified without the writer's authorization. With this knowledge, the user can then decide whether or not to trust applets to perform certain operations, such as accessing files from the hard drive. Using digital signatures is a little complicated. Without going into too much detail, here are the basic steps:

1. Apply to a public certificate authority for a key pair. For a list of CAs, open your browser's security console and look for a category called "signers." Go to the Web site of one of those signers for more information. Two of the more popular are Verisign and Thawte.

2. Create a key database. This is done differently in JDK 1.1 and JDK 1.2. The tool used in JDK 1.1 is called javakey, and is widely thought to be overly complex and buggy. Attempts to fix it actually have made things worse and the version in release 1.1.6 does not work at all. The next release (JDK 1.2) splits this tool into several new tools. The one that manages the key database is called keytool. Documentation for using it is available at http://java.sun.com/products/jdk1.2/docs/
→ guide/security/spec/security-spec.doc6.
→ html.

3. Sign the jar file. This is done by using javakey in JDK 1.1, or jarsigner in JDK 1.2.

This procedure is definitely not for the faint of heart. It is currently very frustrating and not recommended unless you have a real need.

The new JDK, version 1.2, is currently in its third beta. It promises many changes, particularly in the area of GUI components, so it should be interesting to see how this affects the use of Java on the Web. The only new method that has been added to the Applet class is NewAudioClip(), which is a static method, meaning that it can easily be called from other classes.

The Java language must keep evolving to stay current, but should not leave consumers behind or force people to stay on a constant upgrade path. Hopefully the Java Plugin will help to make this possible. The Java Plugin, also called Activator, allows you to embed an applet without using the <APPLET> tag. This means that users must have the plug-in, but it allows the JDK to be switched painlessly. In other words, the user will not have to get a new browser just to run the latest code. If this plug-in becomes widely used, developers will only have to worry about learning new technologies, not targeting browsers.

THE NEW EVENT MODEL

INDEX

Numbers and Symbols

&& characters, 152
   use of in loop statements, 61
*/ (asterisk and slash characters), using in Java
   code, 36
$ (dollar sign), in string variables, 40
= (equal sign), using in code, 39
|| (or) characters, 152
   use of in loop statements, 61
| (pipe) character, using to split up strings, 164
/* (slash and asterisk characters), using in Java
   code, 36
_ (underscore), in string variables, 40

A

Abstract Windowing Toolkit (AWT), 18
ALIGN attribute, APPLET tag, 22-23
alignment values, valid for ALIGN attribute, 23
animation
   controlling with isRunning variable, 127-
     129
   displaying non-stop, 125-126
   double-buffering to stop flickering, 123-124
   making an image move, 120-122
   starting and stopping, 127-129
anonymous inner class, handling a button press
   with in JDK 1.1, 208

Apple Java Developers pages, Web site address
   for, 183
<APPLET></APPLET>tags, 20
   ALIGN attribute, 22-23
   new attributes for in JDK 1.1, 209-210
   using PARAM tag within, 26
applet parameters, Java hierarchical menu
   applet, 173
applet spacing, defining with FlowLayout, 100
applets
   entering and displaying text, 84
   finding on the Internet, 19-28
   freehand drawing in, 74
   hierarchical menu, 161-172
   making them threaded, 120-122
   positioning on Web page, 22-23
   simple calculator, 153-159
   specifying fonts in, 32
   Tic-Tac-Toe, 143-152
   using radio buttons, 87-88
   working with checkboxes, 85-86
   writing your first, 29-38
AppletName.java file, creating in your
   development environment, 12
applets, 4
   changing or setting background color for, 33
   finding on the Internet, 19-28
   specifying fonts for, 32
ARCHIVE attribute, for <APPLET>tag in JDK
   1.1, 209
arrays, using, 51-52

X, Y, Z